BAD REPUBLICAN

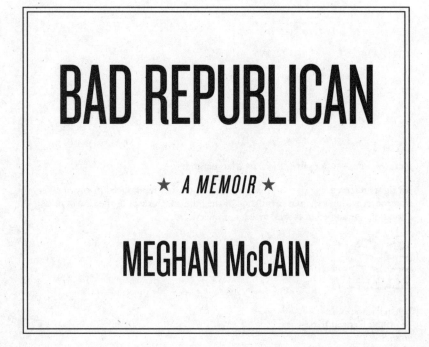

BAD REPUBLICAN

★ *A MEMOIR* ★

MEGHAN McCAIN

BenBella Books, Inc.
Dallas, TX

BenBella Books, Inc.
10440 N. Central Expressway
Suite 800
Dallas, TX 75231
benbellabooks.com
Send feedback to feedback@benbellabooks.com

BenBella is a federally registered trademark.

Printed in the United States of America
10 9 8 7 6 5 4 3 2 1

Library of Congress Control Number: 2021951519
ISBN 9781637742136 (hardcover)
ISBN 9781637742143 (ebook)

Copyediting by Michael Fedison
Proofreading by Lisa Story and Sarah Vostok
Indexing by WordCo Indexing Services
Text design and composition by PerfecType, Nashville, TN
Cover design courtesy of Audible
Cover photo by Emily Shur
Printed by Lake Book Manufacturing

Special discounts for bulk sales are available. Please contact bulkorders@benbellabooks.com.

To Liberty

We have it in our power to begin the world over again.

—Thomas Paine

The world ain't all sunshine and rainbows. It's a very mean and nasty place and I don't care how tough you are, it will beat you to your knees and keep you there permanently if you let it. You, me, or nobody is gonna hit as hard as life. But it ain't about how hard ya hit.

It's about how hard you can get hit and keep moving forward.

—Rocky Balboa

CONTENTS

INTRODUCTION

BAD REPUBLICAN

★ ★ ★

was born in 1984, and I strongly relate to a millennial meme I saw on Instagram:

> *Welcome to your teenage years! Here's a global terrorism event to define your adolescence!*
>
> *Welcome to adulthood! Here's a global recession!*
>
> *Welcome to parenthood! Here's a global pandemic!*
>
> *Don't know about the rest of you, but I'm terrified of middle age.*

In September 2020, I gave birth to my daughter, Liberty Sage. I'd hated being pregnant so much that I'd feared I wouldn't be suited to motherhood or I wouldn't love my baby enough. That fear went away the second the nurse handed her to me. I was instantly filled with an overwhelming, visceral love far beyond anything I'd ever known. Looking at her, I couldn't stop thinking, *Oh my God. Oh my God. Oh my God.* I felt newly connected to the universe and to what it means to be a human being, and I knew I would do anything to protect her. Liberty's birth and my father's death are the two key events creating a before and an after in the story of my life.

At the time, I was filled with new, crippling fears of what might happen if I wasn't with her every second. I was consumed with irrational anxieties about terror attacks and other dangers. They were so vivid that they were paralyzing. Sleeping only in three-hour increments, I entered my own pandemic Twilight Zone—never sure if it was day or night. Talking to my friend on the phone, I said, "What day is it, Monday?" She said, "Close! Thursday." I eventually had to go on medication for postpartum anxiety.

When I returned to *The View* from maternity leave in January 2021, I was happy to see my coworkers, even though we were still virtual, appearing via satellite from wherever they were spending the pandemic. I was alone with my cameraperson in the D.C. bureau.

Every other host who'd had a baby returned to the show in a glow of goodwill, but that was not my experience. Whatever camaraderie we'd established before I left seemed to have evaporated. Joy Behar, my liberal counterpart on the show, said on-air that she hadn't missed me at all. "I did not miss you. Zero." Whoopi Goldberg shot down a riff of mine with an ". . . *Okay*" that went viral. The media had a field day attacking me. The postpartum hormones made me extra sensitive to every slight. It was a very rough reentry.

The pandemic kept dragging on and on, and I wasn't sure when I'd be able to get a vaccine or if anything would ever go back to normal. Not to mention: the January 6 domestic terror attack on the Capitol took place my first week back. Like most Americans, I found it horrific and deeply upsetting.

When Joe Biden won the election, I thought our country—and our show—would enjoy a "Kumbaya" moment of unity. I expected Democrats—particularly those who I worked with—to be over-joyed that Trump was gone. But, if anything, they seemed angrier than ever, squabbling even with one another. The air was thick with tension. I didn't know if it was COVID or the winter weather or the way that even after the Capitol attack, some prominent Republi-cans were refusing to reject QAnon, but my Democratic colleagues seemed more rage-filled in Biden's America than they'd been for the prior four years.

When I was writing this, in the weeks after the inauguration, barbed wire remained all over D.C., where I now live in the Beltway area. The vaccine was being rolled out, but we were still wearing masks, practicing social distancing, and unsure about how much longer the virus would be with us. And certain Republicans seemed to be doubling down on conspiracy theories in a way that tested my belief system.

Antidepressants have been helping me cope with hard-core COVID fatigue and an existential crisis about my political identity. The terror attack, online trolls, volatile mood at my workplace, and pregnancy hormones have combined to make me more scared and more overwhelmed than at any time since my dad died. And back then, I had a lot of support. This time, I feel totally alone.

I'm still a Republican. At the same time, I don't see eye to eye with many in my party when it comes to Trump or old-guard social conservatism. That's why my agent likes to jokingly call me a "bad Republican."

I've come to think that the nickname is kind of perfect. It's unclear how I'd even go about being a "good" Republican these days. If you're not pro-Trump, then, to most of the party, you're a heretic. If you support supposedly liberal policy issues like gay rights and prison reform, which I do, you're seen as not truly conservative. If you haven't completely rejected the party, Lincoln Project–style, then to everyone else, you're considered deeply problematic— especially if you're a pro-life woman, which is seen as being a traitor to your gender.

The good news is that I have a long history as an awkward step-child of the Republican Party. When my father was running for president in 2008, his team found fault with everything from my bleach-blonde hair to my enthusiasm for beer and trashy reality shows. (His campaign staffers had a refrain about me that I likened to *The Sound of Music*'s "How do you solve a problem like Maria?")

Of course, when I started at my current job at *The View* as the only conservative host on a very liberal talk show, I was considered bad simply *because* I was a Republican. I support the military, school choice, freedom of speech, responsible fiscal policy, Israel, and the Second Amendment. I believe taxation is theft, and I'm against cancel culture and hyper-wokeness. I don't believe that *The View* would have hired me today. Nobody as right-leaning as I am would have passed muster.

So, my cohosts dunk on me, and viewers celebrate these little humiliations on Twitter. All that is left for me is to shake it off and keep going. The lesson I've had to learn is that on TV—whether it's a soap opera or a news program—everyone is playing a part. The Republican on a liberal show will always be the adversary. That's the job. You've got to be comfortable with the role of the villain. I've decided to lean into it, to channel Maleficent—who, by the way, deserves her own *Wicked*. Disney princesses might get more applause, but don't we always wonder more about the villains?

CHAPTER 1

LIFE AND LIBERTY

n May of 2019, I was in my first trimester of pregnancy when I agreed to appear on *Late Night with Seth Meyers*. I had morning sickness all day, and my boobs felt like they weighed a thousand pounds. When I put on my bra, it hurt so bad that I yelled in pain. I wanted to cancel, but no one knew I was pregnant, so I couldn't use that as an excuse. My then-publicist said that it was important to keep promoting *The View* and my "brand," whatever that was, even if I wasn't in the mood. I had no expectation that the interview would be easy or simple, but I did think that it would be above-board. That day, I taped two episodes of *The View* and then dragged myself, achy and nauseous, to 30 Rockefeller Center.

From the moment I entered the building, Seth Meyers made me feel uncomfortable. In the bathroom-sized greenroom, he approached me with a phony smile and started up the kind of shallow, schmoozy showbiz conversation that I'm terrible at. When he asked if I had any children, I wondered if he could tell that I'd been throwing up all day.

Once we were out onstage taping, the tension grew much worse. He challenged me to take back something I'd said weeks earlier about what I saw as dangerous comments made by Minnesota representative Ilhan Omar.

At a speech given at the California chapter of the Council on American-Islamic Relations, Omar said: "Far too long we have lived with the discomfort of being a second-class citizen and, frankly, I'm tired of it, and every single Muslim in this country should be tired of it. CAIR was founded after 9/11 because they recognized that some people did something and that all of us were starting to lose access to our civil liberties."

CAIR was founded in 1994, for the record, but of course what's galling here is the line "some people did something." Like a lot of people, I found that dismissive to the point of being grotesque. I get that for me to say anything at all about Ilhan Omar is controversial. There's something about the moment we're in that just me saying her name is enough to make some people start yelling about white privilege. But she is an elected representative, a public figure. It should be okay to critique actions she takes without being called Islamophobic and worse.

She'd said things that I and many others had interpreted as anti-Semitic, too, including: "Israel has hypnotized the world. May Allah awaken the people and help them see the evil doings of Israel." Playing into a Jewish stereotype, she'd tweeted that the U.S. Congress's support for Israel was "all about the Benjamins."

Seth Meyers kept telling me that Omar had apologized for what she'd said and that I should let it go. I said something along the lines of "agree to disagree," but he was having none of it. He kept hitting the same question over and over. To me, it seemed like virtue signaling and like a moment choreographed to go viral. The more awkward I felt, the more he appeared to take in my discomfort.

The studio audience stopped laughing. They sat there in silence. I kept trying to deflect, but he wouldn't let it go. I was confused by why this was so important to him that he would tank the audience experience to make his point.

"Are you her publicist?" I asked.

I would never treat someone that way on my show. In my role as a host, I'll press something twice, but I won't do it more than that if they're not going to play ball or they're going to spin it, because that basically means it's clearly time to move on. And late-night TV is not supposed to be *Meet the Press*. I'd been on *The Tonight Show with Jay Leno* many times, and it had always been fun. I never had the experience of being raked over the coals or mansplained to. But I felt like Seth Meyers was channeling the anger he felt toward Trump onto me. He's one of several snarky white Generation X men in "comedy" who seem to have me on their dartboards. The second anyone who's not a liberal comes on the show, they suddenly act like they're on MSNBC—although my sense is that Rachel Maddow is far classier.

When the interview was over, I sat there for a second, feeling mortified. Seth jumped out from behind his desk and came around to face me. He grabbed my hand and pulled me close to him.

"Tell your mother I said hello," he said, which I thought was bizarre.

I don't remember exactly what I said back—maybe, "What the hell was that?"

I was completely disconcerted and panicked. My heart was racing. I knew those couple of minutes would go viral and that I would see hundreds of antagonistic messages flooding my mentions if I dared look at Twitter.

I vowed then and there not to go on late-night shows ever again. My theory is that these shows get so few non-liberals that whenever they do get one, it's an opportunity to attack them as a symbol of every Republican they don't like. Trump was never going to sit in that chair, so because of my party affiliation, I had to pay for his sins, never mind that I actively spoke out against Trump.

After leaving the studio, I cried in the car on the way back home. I cried when I got home. I cried when I got up the next day. I was obviously hormonal because of the pregnancy, but it was more than that. My feelings were hurt. I didn't want to go onto *The View* for a photo shoot we had scheduled for that day, but I thought if I didn't, everyone would say, "Oh, she couldn't hack it, because she had such a bad appearance on *Seth Meyers*."

So I dragged myself there, and I cried in my dressing room.

I had another fire to put out, too: my husband, Ben—Ben Domenech, who founded the conservative magazine and podcast *The Federalist*—was watching the late-night appearance from home and may have had a few drinks. He rage-tweeted: "I see that @sethmeyers, the untalented piece of shit who only has his job because he regularly gargled Lorne Michaels' balls, went after my wife tonight with his idiotic anti-Semitic bullshit."

I was furious and embarrassed when I saw that. He deleted the tweet, but I stayed mad. I called him in the middle of the night—he was in D.C.—and told him that he was making everything worse.

Backstage at *The View*, I mentioned how he shouldn't have done it.

The woman who does my hair said, "If my spouse did that, I'd think it was hot. He's protecting you. You should give Ben a break."

My makeup artist said the same thing.

"What?" I said. "No! It's bad! He shouldn't be doing that! Did I mention he was drunk?"

Then a crew guy came over to me and said, "Your husband's my hero. Seth Meyers is the worst guy to work with in TV."

Seth's publicist got in touch with me. Apparently, the clip of the show was doing well online, and they were happy about that. I learned that Seth Meyers has poor ratings compared with Stephen Colbert, Jimmy Fallon, and Jimmy Kimmel. In terms of overall late-night-host favorability ratings, he was polling seventh. *Late Night*'s social team was grateful for a rare viral moment. The publicist said that Seth wanted to give me a call.

"No, thank you," I said. "We have nothing else to say to each other."

He'd probably be worried that I'd speak ill of him. He wasn't wrong to worry about that. As the writer Anne Lamott said, "If people want you to write warmly about them, they should have behaved better." Or, to quote Nora Ephron: "Everything is copy."

Seth Meyers ended up writing me a note that was scored into me that said something like: "Dear Meghan, Appreciate you coming on even though it was an away game."

That made me laugh. Every day of my life in New York City, I play an "away game." I'm never surrounded by Republicans. I'm the only conservative *on my own show.*

In good faith, I've gone on many other people's shows and had a great time regardless of our differences. I went on *The Van Jones Show* on CNN for a long, serious interview. He's a very staunch liberal. But we both had a lovely time and even wound up becoming good friends and producing a documentary together. I don't want to be part of a food fight unless it's on my show with people who I know are comfortable with it. Joy and Whoopi and I fight sometimes, but it's consensual. We're paid to disagree, and we have a team of producers helping us navigate our differences. Regardless of how heated it gets, there's a level of trust there, and a fundamental awareness that we're on a team together, with the shared goal of creating a good show for our audience. This was in no way my experience of *Late Night.*

As the photo shoot was about to begin, my doctor called. My latest blood test results were in. My hCG levels weren't rising the way that they should.

I didn't understand what that meant.

She said I might be having a miscarriage and advised me to come right to her office.

Everybody was all set up for the shoot, so I couldn't leave. It took everything I had to stop crying long enough to take the photo. As soon as it was over, I ran to the doctor.

In the examination room, she explained that I was most likely losing my baby.

I couldn't stop crying. I blamed myself.

"I did this media appearance last night that was a disaster, and it's trending all over Twitter and I can't get my blood pressure to go down and I'm so emotional," I told the doctor. "Could my TV appearance last night have done this?"

The doctor told me that the show appearance absolutely did not cause the loss, that being stressed out didn't affect my pregnancy. She pointed out that plenty of women in Syrian war zones have healthy pregnancies.

Still, sitting there, hearing that I was losing my baby while my phone lit up with Twitter notifications—thousands of people posting the clip and fighting over whether I was a "problematic white woman" or Seth Meyers was a dick—easily ranked as one of the worst moments of my life.

To this day, Seth Meyers is one of the very few people who, if I ever saw him in person, I would do everything possible to avoid. Fairly or not, I associate him with having a miscarriage.

To be clear, it wasn't because he was asking me tough questions. I live for tough questions. Go on YouTube. I deal with tough questions all day, every day. It was because he was relentless and petty in front of his audience despite their discomfort. With no regard for anyone else's feelings, he browbeat me about my reaction to an objectively offensive comment and wouldn't move on until I was nearly in tears. This was not a conversation. This was not a debate. He seemed to merely be savoring the experience of lecturing me.

His "away game" comment made me realize that this is why conservatives only go on Fox News, and why people in both communities prefer to interact with people who are like-minded. Though divided as a nation, we are united in the desire not to be yelled at.

I always wanted to know what Seth Meyers got out of our exchange that night. Did it feel good? It's not like it changed anybody's mind about Ilhan Omar. If you want to have a discussion about why you think I'm Islamophobic because I don't like some of the things she said and you want to have a discussion about how what you think I did is wrong in a respectful way, I'm happy to defend myself. I'm not happy to be towed out as a token conservative and then burned in effigy, humiliated for sport.

Mainly, I think it's bad TV.

The only guest I can think of who might have cause to say she left her appearance at *The View* feeling the way I did after *Late Night with Seth Meyers* is the *Baywatch* actress Pamela Anderson.

Last season, we were told that she was coming on to talk about an abusive relationship she'd been in with an old boyfriend. But after Sunny asked her a question about Julian Assange, she wound up arguing his cause so fiercely that I wondered if she might be a proxy for Russian propagandists.

I hate Julian Assange. As far as I'm concerned, WikiLeaks has proven itself to be a serious threat to our national security.

But Pamela Anderson's talking points were straight out of the Kremlin.

I have done a lot of work on behalf of the Magnitsky Act. If you don't know what it is: Sergei Magnitsky was a Russian dissident who was arrested after calling attention to government corruption. He died in a Moscow prison. In his honor, the 2012 Magnitsky Act is a law that blocks anyone who is committing human rights abuses from being able to use the West for slush funds or money laundering. That way, they can't enjoy the fruits of democracy while undermining it.

Julian Assange is a notorious Russian propagandist, so when Pamela Anderson came on the show talking about what a genius he was, I felt I had to say something. "When you were visiting him [Assange], he was allegedly kicked out of the Ecuadorian embassy because he was defecating everywhere and creating messes . . ."

Anderson said, "Well, what would you do if you were in an embassy for six years?"

I said, "I wouldn't be a cyberterrorist—which he is."

Joy backed me up, asking Anderson whether she thought that Julian Assange gave us Trump, because WikiLeaks released Hillary's emails at the worst possible time in the campaign. Anderson responded that *Hillary* was responsible for Trump.

My boss was furious afterward that I'd gone after Pamela Anderson so hard. He didn't think I was being respectful. But I felt like I was bait-and-switched. I was told that I was interviewing her about domestic abuse, and instead, she only wanted to talk about how we should be supporting Julian Assange. But there's no denying that the interview got ugly. There's a picture from that day that people always tweet at me: Pamela Anderson looking at me askance, angry.

So that was a disaster—but I believe it *still* wasn't as creepy as my time on *Seth Meyers.*

Once the miscarriage had begun, my doctor told me there was no way the pregnancy could be preserved, so I had to keep doing my job, ignoring the pain and sense of loss. If you look at the picture taken of me in the photo shoot the day I learned that I was losing the baby, I think you can see that under the glamorous hair and makeup and the well-appointed dressing room set, I'm scared and sad.

The worst part was that I felt so alone in it. After taking two days off work for a D&C—a procedure in which they scrape the remains of the failed pregnancy from the uterus—I returned to this *Daily Mail* headline, attributed to sources inside the show: "EXCLUSIVE: Meghan McCain 'faked sick' to avoid discussing her Trump-supporting father-in-law . . . but was back on air just in time to cozy up to Joe Biden."

Soon after, I wrote an op-ed in the *New York Times* to speak to other women who've experienced pregnancy loss. Without mentioning the late-night debacle, I confessed that I thought I'd done something to cause the miscarriage: "Well, perhaps it was wrong of me to choose to be a professional woman, working in a high-pressure, high-visibility, high-stress field, still bearing the burden of the recent loss of my father and facing on top of that the arrows that come with public life. This is not a complaint. This is reality. I blamed my age; I blamed my personality. I blamed everything and anything a person could think of, and what followed was a deep opening of shame."

It took me a long time and a lot of talking to doctors to realize that miscarriage is common, that it is beyond our control, and that it does not mean that we will not be able to get pregnant again. I felt a sisterhood with all women who, like me, had experienced the joy of pregnancy only to have their hopes dashed.

In December 2019, Joy made a distasteful joke on-air about me breastfeeding a cactus.

I love cacti. I have them around our house to remind me of Arizona. I have an Instagram account called Meghan's Cactus with 46,000 followers where I just post pictures of cacti. I get the reference. But because she knew I'd had a miscarriage, I heard in the joke a cruel implication that the only child I'd ever have was a cactus.

Backstage after the show, I was talking to Abby, who had been a close friend of mine for a very long time. I told her that what Joy said upset me and that I wished Abby had said something in my defense.

"Had the situation been reversed, I would have stuck up for you," I said.

"This is a hard show," Abby said. She seemed surprised that I was so upset, and she apologized.

The following month, Abby left the show because she wanted to work on her dad's Utah gubernatorial campaign. In the media, stories came out recounting our argument about the cactus quip, suggesting that it was why she left. The truth was, she and I were both dealing with a ton of media abuse then, and it was only a matter of time before either or both of us reached a breaking point. I started seriously thinking about my own life span at *The View*, and here's what happened next.

Just a few weeks after that show, I was thrilled to find out that I was pregnant again, but anxious, too. Any twinge in my body made me worry that the pregnancy was failing. I walked around in hope and in fear. When I saw women in their third trimester or babies in strollers, I thought, *I hope that's me one day.*

I was at my doctor's office for an early-pregnancy checkup when I noticed a little sign in the reception area. It read: "Have you traveled recently to China or other parts of Asia?" I thought the question was so strange. The receptionist said I had to answer it, and I said, "No, why?"

She said there was a virus spreading through China.

The next day at *The View*, when we were pitching what we call "Hot Topics," I said, "I keep hearing about this virus in China. I think we should discuss it."

The consensus was that it wouldn't come to the United States and we shouldn't be paranoid.

Then, in early February, Ben and I were out to dinner with a friend of ours and his wife. His wife is Chinese. She told me at dinner that her brother, who lives in China, was quarantined, apart from his family.

"What the hell is quarantine?" I said.

She said, "It means you can't leave the house because there's this weird, highly communicable virus."

I was instantly scared. I grew up watching the 1995 movie *Outbreak*, and I've always feared the Ebola virus.

I leaned across the dinner table and said, "If that shit can happen there, that shit can happen here!"

"Should we be taking the subway?" I asked Ben on the way home. "Should we be extra freaked out because I'm pregnant?"

We decided to try to keep everything normal for as long as we could, but to stay as close to home as possible until we knew more.

Everything changed rapidly after that day. My days at *The View* got weirder and weirder as everyone else began asking the same questions Ben and I were asking.

At the time, *The View* was shot in a gigantic studio, rather like the World Wrestling Entertainment's arena, a Greco-Roman amphitheater, or the cage-match Thunderdome in *Mad Max*, with hundreds of seats in concentric circles.

As news of the mysterious illness spread, the audience grew smaller and smaller. Crew members began calling in sick. There were signs that the virus was more dangerous for older people, and Joy, at the age of seventy-seven, said she didn't feel safe in the studio anymore. Hand sanitizer was even going missing backstage. I got in trouble for putting a photo on Instagram of a bottle of hand sanitizer, taped to a mirror, on which someone had written, "Is it worth losing your job if you steal this?"

Whoopi was the next to ask to work from home because her immune system was compromised. She'd almost died the year before from pneumonia and sepsis, and her lungs hadn't fully recovered.

I didn't know what to do. I wanted to be brave. I've always been a show-must-go-on, play-hurt, tough-it-out kind of person. I decided that if they weren't canceling the show, I wasn't going to take myself out of the studio. I would keep showing up for work until they told me not to. And yet, I grew increasingly afraid that I would catch the virus.

Ben got angrier and angrier that no one at work seemed particularly worried about protecting my pregnancy. There wasn't a lot of information yet about how the virus affected pregnant women. Ben and I wondered if my catching COVID could hurt the baby or cause me to miscarry. I felt very scared every time I left my apartment.

At that time, I had two bosses. One was James Goldston, the president of ABC News; the other, Barbara Fedida, a senior VP who has since been fired for racially insensitive comments in the workplace. (She once said of Robin Roberts that the network wasn't "asking her to pick cotton.")

When I told her I was pregnant, she congratulated me, but when I asked her if I should start working from home, she said no, and: "We're all going to feel very silly when this is over."

"But people are dying," I said. "Doesn't it seem dangerous? I feel we should take this seriously."

"Nope, we're going to keep working," she said. "We're essential workers. We're a news show. People are counting on us. We need to buck up!" She said it was my "duty to keep coming in."

I wanted to show up, to "be brave for the world," but I also wanted to take care of myself.

Being pregnant felt like a liability in this circumstance. If it were only about me, I would have kept going. I'd worked sick a million times. If anything, I was sometimes accused of being *too* tough. I didn't want pregnancy to take that away. But now, when it came to the decision about whether to go to work, for the first time in my life, I had to think about someone other than myself.

Ben, always sensible, told me that we didn't know enough about the virus, and ABC didn't know enough either. He said we shouldn't take Barbara's word for it being safe. We had to talk to a medical professional to get more informed advice. I went in to see my doctor and explained the situation.

"Look," the doctor said, "honestly, right now no one knows enough about this. But it's becoming increasingly clear that this virus is bad and unpredictable. It is my professional opinion that if you can avoid going into the studio, you should. And if you can get out of the city for a while, even better."

I called my executive producer Brian Teta and told him what the doctor said. He responded, "I completely understand and agree that it's the best thing for you to work from home until we know more." He was very generous about the whole thing. Producers at ABC sometimes get a bad rap, but Brian is a great leader, cool under pressure. He's always served as a constant source of support, and he was especially heroic in those scary early days of the pandemic.

And so I became the third host to start working from home, after Joy and Whoopi.

Ben and I packed bags in our apartment and called my dad's old driver to ask if he'd be willing to drive us to Virginia, where we have a house. I figured we could ride out the pandemic as long as it lasted—my outside estimate was three weeks—and then go back to our apartment and back to the Thunderdome. I spent the whole drive wondering if I was overreacting and making a huge mistake. I worried I was being a wuss.

But by the time we'd been in Virginia for a few days, I'd learned that a bunch of people at ABC had gotten sick, including some who worked at *The View*. In the weeks that followed, a couple of ABC employees died, and everything started to feel more and more apocalyptic. On Twitter, I saw a video of body bags being put into a refrigerated truck, of old people dying en masse in Italy, of empty city streets. It felt like no one knew what was going on.

I'd hoped to keep my pregnancy a secret longer, especially because I felt the risk of miscarriage was still high, but people wanted to know why someone as young as me would be "self-isolating," as they were phrasing it then. And so, my March pregnancy announcement became all about COVID: "I consulted with my doctors and they advised me that for the safety of our baby and myself, I should be extra vigilant about limiting the amount of people we come in contact with."

Sequestered at home, I taped *The View* in the morning. Ben and I played *Mario Kart* and watched *Tiger King*. Unable to see friends, I quickly grew depressed. One friend wanted to throw me a Zoom baby shower, but I thought that would only remind me of how much I was missing, so I declined. Had I known my last lunch with my girlfriends was going to be the last lunch I'd have in a restaurant for a year, I would've chosen something fancier than Momofuku noodles.

Every week, I checked a pregnancy app to see what size the baby should be and what I should know. Now the app was full of reports about COVID. Early reports suggested that pregnant women were at higher risk for severe illness, death, and preterm labor.

I was thoroughly freaked out. I stayed at my house. I didn't leave the neighborhood for any reason, for months. Very early each morning, I'd take a trip alone to a local park, where I'd walk around feeling cold and sad and lonely. For months, I was not excited to be pregnant, only fearful. My baby felt like a burden. I didn't think I could roll with the punches of this type of emergency situation the way I could have if I hadn't been pregnant. I wasn't sure I could be there for her while also dealing with everything in the world. I felt like a burden on Ben and everyone else. It was the worst time to be pregnant. There was so much more to worry about.

Meanwhile, a lot of people on Twitter were letting me know in no uncertain terms that they were mad that I never shared a pregnant photo. I wished I could tell them that when all of this was over, I looked forward to celebrating with them, but that in the moment,

I was struggling. I felt too vulnerable to deal with what I knew would be a lot of vicious comments if I did share private photos. I wrote on social media: "Given that people write on photos I put up of my family they are glad my Dad got cancer and he's in hell, I thought I would leave my unborn child out of the social media cesspool as much as possible."

At the same time, many people did support me in my attempt to keep the pregnancy private, and I'm forever grateful to them.

Doctor visits didn't help my anxiety level. I'd always imagined Ben would be next to me as we saw our baby move around on the ultrasound and heard her heartbeat, but because of COVID, I had to go to my appointments alone. Everyone wore masks. Hand sanitizer sat on every table. It felt like patients were rushed in and out as fast as possible and with the minimum amount of touching. I didn't love being touched by strangers, so that part was okay, but there was no pleasure in the milestones of pregnancy, only anxiety.

I began having pep talks with my baby in the womb, telling her she'd have to be tough. I told her that the world she'd be entering would be far from peaceful, far from what I'd hoped it would be by the time she arrived.

Then came labor.

I'd heard scary stories about C-sections, so I was determined to have a natural, vaginal birth. Cut to thirty hours of labor later, I was shouting, "Do whatever the hell you have to do! I just need this to end!"

I begged for an epidural.

"Come on," a nurse said, patting on my arm. "You need to push through."

My whole body felt like it was being ripped apart. I had been "pushing through" for a million hours.

"I'm a tough girl," I said to the nurse. "Why are you making me feel like this is a contest? Like if I don't do this the right way, I've failed?"

"I never had an epidural," she said. "I gave birth naturally to all three of my children."

We are not the same person! I thought. *We are different people! Why does it have to be as difficult as possible to count? Why does it have to hurt so much for you to tell me I'm doing a good job? And would you ever say something like that to a man? If Ben was getting a vasectomy, would you tell him, "C'mon, you're tough! You don't need anesthesia!"*

"I don't know if you know anything about me," I said when I caught my breath between contractions. "Nobody thinks I'm not tough. I have nothing to prove to you. Give me the motherfucking epidural."

I got the epidural and was finally able to stop wanting to die. A few hours later, they said labor wasn't progressing fast enough, so they took me for an emergency C-section. I was relieved that I was finally going to meet my baby.

Liberty Sage McCain Domenech was born on Monday, September 28, 2020, at 8:38 p.m. It felt much later. I'd have sworn it was past midnight. The doctors offered music in the delivery room, so I requested the Beach Boys, my dad's favorite. He'd died two years earlier, and that band reminded me of him all the time, especially the song Liberty was born to: "Don't Worry Baby."

When they pulled her out, I couldn't see her at first because they had a curtain up. I couldn't hear her either. She didn't scream.

I did not take the song's cue not to worry. I worried a lot. After a few moments of silence that felt like hours, I frantically yelled, "Why isn't she crying? Is something wrong?"

A kind nurse said, "Just give her a second, Mom."

Then I heard her. She wasn't loud, like in the movies. She wasn't shrill. She gave the softest, sweetest little cry, almost as if she were pronouncing the word "Wah."

When I saw her, at last, in the nurse's arms, it was as if I'd always known her.

I felt something I'd never felt before—a surge of perfect love and also tremendous responsibility. She wasn't there, and then she was. And she looked at once nothing and everything like I'd expected her to. Ben is Puerto Rican and has dark, curly hair. I'd imagined her resembling him. But she looked much more like me, and even more like my mother.

Look at you! I thought. *You're a real person!*

It felt like a miracle. The euphoria of motherhood was the most intense, overwhelming, amazing sensation I've ever had. It was almost like my dad was reincarnated; Liberty had his smile. A piece of my heart broke when he died. With her birth, she healed it.

CHAPTER 2

SHAKING WITH RAGE

Right after labor, I felt more than ready to leave the hospital with Ben and Liberty. I couldn't wait for us to start our life together. But because of the C-section, I had to stay there for at least two days. They came back in to check on me every sixteen seconds. With the beeping and the lights, I felt like I was in a sleep-deprivation experiment.

In the recovery room, two hours after I'd given birth, I began to drift off at last. I'd been up for more than thirty-eight hours at that point. Another nurse came in and said brightly, "If you think you're going to sleep, you're not!" She wanted me to start trying to breastfeed.

"I just labored for thirty hours," I said. "I have to sleep a little first."

"Fine," she said. "I'll come back in two hours."

Two hours later, there she was, trying to get me to breastfeed. The first thing that comes out of your breasts is colostrum, a magical substance full of antibodies and other wonderful, life-giving properties. Liberty was not interested. She screamed. She wouldn't latch. I started crying, too.

The nurse said things that made it sound as though without breastfeeding, my daughter wouldn't be as healthy or as smart as she would be otherwise, and I wouldn't bond with her.

I was so drugged out from the C-section that when they said she was losing weight, I thought that might mean she was extremely sick.

"You're not producing enough breast milk," the nurse said. "So, what do you think about her supplementing?"

"What does that mean?" I said.

"Giving her formula," she responded.

"Well, what would you do?" I asked.

"I don't know," she said. "I breastfed all of my children."

As a rule, I love nurses, and I am sure the couple who I felt judged by were good people and had my best interests at heart. That said, the exchanges I had with this one about breastfeeding were extremely awkward.

I interview people for a living. I know a lot about body cues and tone of voice and verbs that people use when they're trying to dodge something or they're trying to manipulate me.

I said I thought we should give Liberty formula so she wouldn't starve while I figured out the breastfeeding thing.

I felt defeated, like I was going to harm my baby on day one because her diet had to be supplemented with formula. Apparently, every other mother this nurse saw gave birth naturally in a sun-dappled meadow, with songbirds landing on their shoulders. On nothing but the purest of breast milk, their babies grew instantly fat and strong, and a rainbow appeared. And now here I was with my epidural and my C-section and my failure to latch.

I'm used to having control in situations, feeling empowered, feeling strong. In my workplace, I feel respected and valued. But in that hospital room, none of that mattered. What I heard was: "You're a huge failure if you can't correctly position your nipple."

If it weren't for COVID, maybe I'd have taken all the usual parenting and birth classes and I would have been more prepared. But I guess I thought the doctors and nurses have done it enough—they could guide us and help us figure it all out. As it was, I had so many voices in my head in those first few days. Every six hours, there was a new nurse on duty. Some were lovely, but others made me feel lousy.

Determined to do the right thing, I talked to several lactation coaches. Most of them were wearing pink scrubs with pink masks. One kept pouring formula all over my tits, attempting to get Liberty to latch. Screaming, she would latch for a second and then pull away, with formula all over her face and all over my boobs. It was like a horror movie, only with milk instead of blood. Another consultant yelled at me to squeeze my boob and "make a hamburger!" out of it. I tried and tried, but whatever meal I was serving up with my breast-origami, Liberty was having none of it.

Two days after childbirth, I developed postpartum preeclampsia, a dangerous condition in which your blood pressure shoots up after birth and there's excess protein in your urine. Untreated, it can cause seizures or even a stroke. I was told I had to stay at the hospital longer and I had to go on a magnesium drip, which can cause confusion, drowsiness, and excessive sweating. Later, I would learn that it can take time for your milk to come in, and stress can delay it.

I desperately wanted to go home. I tried to talk the doctors into letting me go. Then I talked to my mom. She had a stroke before she was fifty and has high blood pressure, so she said, "You have to take it seriously. It's only a couple more days. Just stay there and get the drip." And so, I stayed.

Throughout it all, Ben was great. He spent hours holding Liberty, who they brought back and forth from the nursery in one of those room-service carts. He tried to reassure me that everything was okay, and he never left my side—except for once. Sometime in the night a few days in, he got off the uncomfortable bench they had him sleeping on and said to me, "I can't get any sleep. I'm going to go sleep in the car in the parking lot for a couple of hours, and then I'll be back." I nodded and fell back asleep.

Soon after, a nurse woke me up and said, "Your husband has gone and left you, so we have to put the baby in the nursery."

Between the magnesium and the lack of sleep and the frayed nerves, I said, "My husband *left* me? I just gave birth to our child!"

In that moment, I believed that I had been abandoned and that, therefore, they were taking my child to be raised by another woman.

I tried to call Ben, but he was sleeping peacefully at last in the leaned-back front seat of his car and didn't pick up. I started panicking. I called my sister-in-law, hysterical.

"The nurses say Ben left me!" I wailed.

"I will figure this out and do whatever you need," she said, which is the exact right thing to say to a postpartum woman, regardless of the circumstance. She called Ben, who by this point had woken up, and she sorted it all out. There had been no abandonment. He returned to the room, and so did Liberty.

Unfortunately, that moment didn't do wonders for my blood pressure, which would not come down no matter what medications they were pumping into me. I couldn't leave until I could get my blood pressure down. And I couldn't get my blood pressure down, I was convinced, because I was *full of rage*.

My final day at the hospital, the morning I was finally to be allowed to leave, the doctors and nurses came in and found me smiling. I was so happy we could finally go home. We had packed my bag, and I had finally taken a shower. I looked almost human. I felt optimistic and free. I was ready to go out into the world with my baby.

"Your blood pressure is still too high," a doctor said. "You can't leave."

At this, I had a total, cataclysmic meltdown. I started hysterically crying. "I'm never leaving this hospital!" I wailed. "Never! Liberty is going to grow up here! I will grow old in this room!" Irrational and panicked, I became consumed with the fear that I would never be strong enough to take care of her and that she'd be taken away from me.

Finally, I calmed down enough to say to anyone who would listen: "I know myself and my body because I do physically, mentally, and emotionally exhausting things publicly a lot. And part of how I keep my stamina up is by staying hydrated and eating right and getting a ton of sleep. After giving birth and having a C-section, I need so much more rest, and I'm just not getting it here. I'm not going to get healthy having forty-five minutes to sleep every night and not eating right and feeling emotionally whipsawed. Plus, COVID! If we stay in this hospital longer, don't we increase our chances of getting it?"

The doctor said, "I can't let you leave. It's just not good medicine."

I kept lobbying to go home. Lobbying and crying, for all I was worth.

At last, the doctor said I could leave if I upped my blood pressure medication and monitored my vital signs closely. Before they let me leave, they made us watch videos about parenting. I wasn't sure why they were throwing this remedial education at me. I suspected they thought I needed the tutoring, especially after the nurse gave me her inspiring last words of wisdom: "When you order yourself lunch, make sure it's healthy."

On my way out, I found myself trying to convince her that I was an independent person: "I've done a lot of things in life. I'm accomplished. I can order lunch."

The question I was left with after my labor, delivery, and week in the hospital: *Why are we doing this to women?* My first experience as a mother was that of insecurity and failure. Back at home, where all three of us were sleeping well and eating well and far happier, I grew angry about what I'd been through.

It took me a while to get to the place where I felt like it was the right time to become a mother. At thirty-five, I was that cliché career woman who waited until I was in a good spot professionally, and until I was married. And I had to mourn a miscarriage first.

Delivering a healthy baby should have been a victory and a moment of joy, not an opportunity for criticism.

Once I was home with medication, my blood pressure gradually came down, though I had to test it every few hours. The breastfeeding started to work well, and I felt far more in control. A few weeks in, I developed mastitis, painful inflammation of the mammary gland, but I kept pumping, and it worked out. Ben and I took shifts with Liberty so that we could each have an hour here or there to do other things (for example, I used that time to write this). And I felt like the scales fell away from my eyes. I wanted to shout it from the rooftops that the way we talk to women about this is a big lie.

The fact that women aren't guaranteed paid maternity leave for twelve weeks is abhorrent, shameful, and embarrassing. You're given no support, not even if you develop preeclampsia, or fail to latch, or if your baby's crying all the time, or if you get mastitis (I've had it twice now). I'm not used to having to ask anyone for help, ever. But since becoming a mother, I've had to ask for help a lot.

I felt so vulnerable that I needed physical help. Right after giving birth, I couldn't do anything on my own. My sister-in-law had to help me shower and eat. The physical recovery from the C-section was much more painful than I anticipated. It completely took me out at the knees, and I'm not used to things taking me out at the knees.

I was also extremely grateful for Ben. Now that he had become a father, I was seeing him in a whole new light. He grew up in a large, close family, so when Liberty was born, he knew how to change her diapers right away, whereas I had to learn. He's understanding and helpful and has saved me time and time again.

On Instagram, I posted:

Today is the last day of 2020 and tomorrow is the love of my life's birthday. I don't know what I would do without you Ben. You and Liberty are the best things that have ever happened to me. This year has brought us even closer together (which I didn't think was possible). You have the most brilliant political mind and were way ahead of the curve on what so many Americans were feeling this year and had the guts to call it out before anyone else would. I am constantly in awe of your instincts, grit, courage and the voice you give to the underrepresented in the country. You are the most loving, supportive, nurturing husband I could dream of and my constant teammate and partner no matter what chaos is thrown at us. There is nothing sexier than watching you become a father. I love the way Liberty responds to your voice. It's like you have a secret language you speak to one another. Thank you for keeping both of our hearts wild and never dulling the flame. I know someday we will leave for the mountains together old, grey, and feral and never return. Until then, happy early birthday baby

I immediately heard from female friends of mine how lucky I was that my husband did *anything*. One had just lost her nanny and was panicking.

"You're going to be fine!" I said. "Ben and I figured out that if we take it in shifts, we don't wear out as quickly. When I'm pumping, he walks her around, and when he needs to work, I watch her; then we switch."

"That won't work for me," my friend said. "My husband doesn't think it's his responsibility as a man."

I tried to be understanding, but in the back of my head, I thought, *That would not fly in my house.* I'm horrified by stories about men who think it's emasculating or it's not their role to do basic childcare.

I give thanks that I have Ben. I couldn't do this alone. How single moms do this is beyond me, much less any woman with more than one child. And yet, even in this enviable situation—I love Ben and we're happily married and he's great at changing diapers—sometimes he will look after Liberty for forty-five minutes and then he'll say, "I'm so tired."

"You do not know tired!" I respond. "You get to sleep straight through the night, and I have to wake up every three hours!"

The truth is that having a new baby in the house is hardest on mothers, but genuinely exhausting for everyone. Every half hour, there's something that must be done. I'm pumping or feeding her or putting her down or changing her, and then the cycle restarts. In between, somehow, I need to shower, eat, work. Every moment of my life is spent extracting things out of my body or putting things in. I'm looking at the clock now, and it's 6:24 p.m. Wasn't it 7:00 a.m. two minutes ago?

Spending all day every day with her for the first few weeks of her life has been magical, but also a roller coaster.

One moment, I'm staring at her and thinking she's an angel sent from heaven.

Then, ten minutes later, she won't stop crying, and I'm in the fetal position, wailing, *What do I doooo?*

And ten minutes after *that*, I'm looking at the color of her hair and crying because it's so beautiful.

New motherhood is how I imagine it is to do Ecstasy at Burning Man. It's glorious, but everyone's in weird outfits, and it doesn't quite feel real. Also, it's hard to stay hydrated.

Motherhood answered every existential question I ever had, but at the same time, it feels as though you're going to be punished. You're not 100 percent available in all ways to all people, and there's no room for it.

Picture-perfect-Pinterest parents now fill me with resentment. I am willing to believe that some women just naturally look great after giving birth—Hilaria Baldwin, for example—but especially in the West, we put an irrational amount of pressure on new mothers to look amazing. I saw one celebrity photo on Instagram that haunted me. Days after giving birth, the woman was wearing full makeup and an evening gown. Her husband was in a suit. In another picture soon after, she was wearing skintight leather pants. In my breast-milk-stained pajamas, from my bed, I started to think, based on what I was seeing on social media, that I was the only person whose body didn't miraculously bounce back a week postpartum.

If at any time in the first month after giving birth someone had said to me, "Meghan, put on these leather pants," I would have looked at them like they'd told me to do a triple axel in ice skates.

You know what I looked like after I gave birth? Jabba the Hutt. I was *not* glowing. I was giant and blotchy and exhausted.

When I saw this picture of this celebrity and her husband all dressed up, I finished pumping, and I woke Ben up.

"Do you wish you were with a woman like this?" I said, thrusting my phone in his groggy face. "Would you be happier? Do you want us to be this family?"

Yes, it was a loaded question. But even in his bleariness, he gave the right answer.

"No," he said, "because I don't want to put on a tuxedo right now." He also said something I'd been asking myself: "Who is this picture for?"

I know he was only saying this to make me feel better, but I felt vindicated. *Who are these pictures for?* Because in that moment, it felt like they were there purely to make me feel bad.

And oh, I felt bad. It was the first time post-birth that I was truly insecure about my body. I wondered if Liberty would be mad later that we didn't take any beautiful professional pictures with her as a newborn. I wondered if I'd be hotter to my husband if I'd put on fake eyelashes and leather pants a week after my C-section.

As it was, I didn't put on makeup for weeks and weeks. I looked like hell. I was barely showering. The only person I saw online showing any images from new motherhood that felt real was Amy Schumer. I was so heartened by those pictures of her breast-pumping, looking exhausted. That's how I felt.

Still, I dwelt on the glamorous celebrity's photos for days. I sent them to my friends and said, "I don't understand how this is physically possible."

One made me feel better by saying: "The message those pictures send is that as women, you're supposed to not take a second after something so intense as birth to rest. There's no room to look like shit. Or feel like shit. Or heal."

In theory, I agreed with that. But the more I looked around online, the more images I saw that made me feel bad. Another woman put up an Instagram story in which she returned home from the hospital to giant gold balloons that said her day-old son's name on them and a bottle of Dom Pérignon on the kitchen table with the world's fanciest brunch laid out—I'm talking raspberries-sprinkled-over-orange-slices fancy.

I'd returned home from the hospital in grubby sweatpants. I could barely walk up the stairs. There was no food. We had dirty laundry in the hamper.

I put lipstick on for Thanksgiving, and as I was putting Liberty to bed, I accidentally got lipstick on her crib and all over her. I don't understand how these new moms are able to put on full faces of makeup and keep them on long enough to take a picture.

And I know at least some of them aren't Photoshopped because one Instagram goddess and I have a mutual friend who went to her house soon after she had her baby. Of this woman, my friend said: "She looks incredible! She doesn't have a hair out of place!"

When this friend came to my house, I opened the door wearing a gray sweatshirt through which my boobs had slowly begun to leak milk. As the circles of wetness engulfed more and more of my top, I excused myself to change. My hair was out of place, and I suspect she did not tell our other friend that I looked incredible.

I believe it's detrimental and toxic to pretend it's easy to be a new mother. I haven't put one picture up of myself during maternity leave because I haven't gotten out of my sweatpants in a million years. I look like I got in an accident. I thought I would be back at work in four weeks. Then with the C-section, I couldn't even carry things for the first couple of weeks.

On my Instagram and my Twitter, viewers keep writing, "When are you coming back? You've taken long enough!"

I wanted to say: *That's flattering, but my C-section scar is still healing. My body's shot to hell.* I had the most excruciating back pain I've ever had in my entire life. Plus, I was sweating to death through my sheets every night—sweating so much it was like I had just stepped out of a shower. Have you ever seen an orca in captivity? Its fin falls. It looks sad. That's how my breasts look to me now: Sad. Accusatory. "We were good to you!" they seem to be saying. "Why did you do this to us?" My stomach now has stretch marks and what I can only describe as a shelf of fat that no amount of shapewear can hide.

I googled old party photos because I wanted to see what my boobs used to look like. They'll never look that way again because they're so wrecked now by breastfeeding, but at least they had their day in the sun. In preparing to go back to *The View*, I texted the show's stylist and said, "Do you have a good bra? A *magical* bra?"

I might want to have another baby one day, but I need to take a beat. I don't know how women have them one after the other. My body couldn't take it. How ungrateful I used to be for the life I used to have, I was telling my friend. "I'm two *Housewives* episodes behind for the first time in my life because I don't have time to watch them. I couldn't survive twins. I would be dead. I would say to them, 'I died to give you both life. I love you. Bye.'"

We can't have it all. That whole fantasy was a lie. I wasn't aware of how much I had been lied to until I became a mother. I'm the luckiest woman on planet Earth, and in the first month I was home after giving birth, I didn't leave my house except to go to the pediatrician. I was so overwhelmed. I would try to do a Zoom meeting in the five minutes she was asleep, and I'd think, *I don't know how women do this*. I don't think we can do it all, at least not without a lot of support or no sleep, and I don't think we should tell women that they can.

Shame on our culture for putting pregnant women in this situation. I have every advantage: I have savings. My husband is involved. My incredibly sweet mother-in-law comes over sometimes to help. But it's still so hard. What does everyone else do?

If it's this hard for me, think about policewomen, nurses, and teachers. How are they returning to work in a month? How are they finding space and support to pump if they're trying to breastfeed? What if they can't take a month off and still pay their rent? If a woman like me, with financial means and a fancy job, is struggling this hard, the average woman is drowning.

I don't think it's a government-handout mandate. I don't think it's all the clichés that conservatives have used to not enact it. I'm the last person to say, "Write a check as an answer to a problem in society." But part of the breakdown of our culture, in my opinion, is the breakdown of family. We, as a culture, are not giving families space to become families. If you're working a minimum-wage job and get no paid family leave, what exactly in the hell are you supposed to do?

I obviously take my career seriously, and I want to work. But how can I do my job and also take care of my two-month-old baby? I can't even get my hair highlighted because it takes five hours to get it done, including travel, and the breast pump that I use doesn't work well enough for me to get enough milk to cover that. The last time I left to take Liberty to the doctor, there was no way to feed her or pump for a couple of hours, and by the time we got home, it felt as though my boobs were going to explode. It was awful.

Now, I don't like being told that because I'm a woman, I should vote for a woman, period, but maybe when it comes to this issue, there's no other option. Our country's failure to look after new mothers is a good example of something that might be better if there were more women in power. And anyone who says that women are incapable of leadership has never seen how hard a new mother works.

Maternity leave should be a bipartisan issue. Shame on every lawmaker who hasn't passed something significant in this country. If we can spend billions of dollars on national defense, then we can spend money to let women have a break when they have a baby, period. All women. It shouldn't be this agonizing and stressful.

I was very arrogant about motherhood before becoming a mother. I was dismissive of moms in a way that I now know was unkind. I used to judge quite harshly. If women complained about how hard it was, I would think, *Whatever. Pull it together.* Now I think, *My God! How does any mother find time to put her pants on?*

On some level, I'm embarrassed to say that when I was younger, I believed what I'd heard about how women who become stay-at-home mothers just aren't ambitious. Society does not respect stay-at-home moms nearly enough.

When I was twenty-one, I worked at *Newsweek* magazine. One of the editors who'd just had a baby would go into her office and pump. My friend and I would make fun of the loud noise the pump made. That friend and I were talking the other day, and I told him, "I need to write a deep apology letter to that editor for being such a shitty person back then." The truth is, I am profoundly sorry. I was an asshole and an idiot. And, proving that karma is real, seventeen years later, I'm keeping my husband from sleep with the loud sound of this pump attached to my breasts.

Saudi Arabia—where they don't let women vote or wear tank tops—gives women ten weeks of paid leave. Canada pays women more than half of their wages for fifteen weeks. Italy gives women five months. Why do we have nothing but, for certain companies, a guarantee that you can take twelve unpaid weeks off without being fired?

Even *The View* doesn't pay women for maternity leave, which I find pretty appalling, especially for such a progressive, feminist, pro-woman show. By contrast, Fox News pays for four months of maternity leave. I envied my friends at Fox who didn't even have to think about taking time with their new babies. For all its flaws, Fox is a family company.

And while, for me, losing that income was not a make-or-break situation, I worried about what losing those paychecks does to others at the company. My producer, who is ten years younger than me, was pregnant at the same time I was. Her baby was born right before mine. It's one thing for a host of *The View* not to be paid maternity leave (and I know for a fact they didn't pay former host Abby Huntsman either). It's another thing for young people, for whom taking weeks off work with no pay adds a huge amount of anxiety at an already stressful time. People at the network have been complaining about this situation for years, and nothing's ever been done about it. When I became pregnant, I felt it was a burden.

Michelle Obama has said, "That whole 'so you can have it all.' Nope, not at the same time." Nothing rings truer to me than that. That's why I think *Lean In* is such bullshit. If you're not a CFO of a major company, you don't have the flexibility or the support to seize that kind of power. Other cultures foster women and children so much better than we do. Across the board, women in this country are being lied to. Conservatives emphasize the family. Why aren't we taking care of families? Liberal movie stars perpetuate the myth that your fertility will be there for you forever and that motherhood is glamorous. I love this country so much, but I believe that we, as Americans, punish women for having children.

Becoming a mother, it was as if a veil had been lifted. I suddenly saw at once how deeply privileged I was and also so clearly how much this country doesn't do for women.

I started doing research on how other cultures deal with childbirth and new mothers. In Japan and China, women don't leave their house for a month; family members arrive to take care of them. In India, whole families move in with them to help.

If I had to do it over again, I'd have more of a birth plan, and I'd make sure I told Ben exactly what I wanted him to tell the nurses. I'd also hire a doula who would be on my side so I didn't have to advocate for myself while trying to do the hardest physical work of my life.

I would tell a woman before she goes into labor: "Okay, so you're going to be asked to breastfeed immediately after. And if you don't want to breastfeed, tell them X. If your milk doesn't come in but you want to nurse, do Y. They're all fine options." I always hate it when women are made to feel bad about anything. It's one of the things that has bonded me and united me to my cohosts and the women in *The View* audience. None of us likes being told what to do.

I would emphasize that if you're not breastfeeding for whatever reason, not to worry so much. It's not as if you won't bond with your baby. My adopted little sister, Bridget, came to us when she was ten weeks old. My mother obviously did not breastfeed her. Does that mean my sister never properly bonded to my mother? Of course not. She's as close to us as any of our siblings.

On top of everything else women have to deal with on a daily basis, it's multiplied a thousandfold by motherhood. (And I can tell you from experience, if you are following a path of childlessness into your thirties, that can entail some serious judgment, too.)

For women of color, all of this is much worse. The statistics about fetal and maternal mortality for Black women are chilling. If you read Serena Williams's birth story, you will see that she almost died. And that the only reason she didn't is because she insisted that the doctor look for blood clots because she knew the danger due to her past medical history. Why wouldn't the doctor have done this as a matter of course? Why do women—even *Serena Williams*, one of the toughest athletes in the entire world—have to lobby to be treated with basic consideration?

I don't want any other woman to experience what I did. The entire time I was trying to bond with my newborn daughter, I felt I needed to justify my career and my life choices to people I don't know. It seemed to me only the latest example of how women are treated differently and worse. Women on television, women in politics, women in business—it's always the same story. Everyone wants to tell you how you're screwing up.

Right around the time I was being told to "push through," Jeffrey Toobin was masturbating on a work Zoom with his *New Yorker* colleagues and then calling it a "stupid mistake." Again and again, I see men being given pass after pass while a woman who raises her voice is called a "psycho bitch." I was led to believe women would be treated as equals by now. We're not. If the future is female, the future feels very far away.

CHAPTER 3

WHAT REALLY HAPPENS BACKSTAGE

I n July of 2017, when I was thirty-two, my father was diagnosed with a rare form of brain cancer. I immediately left my broadcast job at Fox News. It felt like too much of a conflict to work for a place that was pro-Trump even as Trump was obsessively taunting my sick father. And any thoughts about my career were drowned out by the knowledge that my father might not have much longer to live. I wanted to spend as much time with him as possible.

I kept my apartment in New York, but for all intents and purposes, I was back living at home with my parents in Arizona, where my new job was to help take care of my dad. I woke up at five in the morning and took him to chemo, and all day, I did whatever he needed. I went to Whole Foods to get groceries, took him to his doctor's appointments, cooked his meals, kept him company. When he felt up to it, we'd go for a walk or play with the dogs. I was tired all the time. The most exhausting thing was trying to keep on a game face for him.

My parents were alternating between their condo in Phoenix and their ranch in Sedona, depending on my dad's work and treatment schedules. In the evening, he liked to watch sports or whatever old Western was on the Grit network. We'd sit out on the deck and have a drink and listen to music. He had a playlist of songs by Frank Sinatra, Glen Campbell, the Beach Boys, ABBA, John Denver, the Mamas & the Papas. Weirdly, he loved music that was popular when he got out of prison, including a lot of anti-war songs. I think the songs reminded him of times in his life when he loved freedom the most.

Those days weren't glamorous, but they were rewarding and humbling—not unlike taking care of a baby, I would later learn.

Initially, my father had lied to me about what he had, saying it was "a melanoma on his head that needed radiation." That didn't sound right. Finally, I got my mother to agree to tell me what it really was. She texted me: "glioblastoma."

Googling, I saw that it was a deadly form of brain cancer with a median survival time of nine to fourteen months. I told my mom that I couldn't believe they were ever thinking of trying to hide that. She said, "Meghan, a doctor from the Mayo Clinic drove to our house to tell your dad that he was going to die soon. He was not processing it, and so he was saying all kinds of things."

A week later, my dad and I were at a medical office together when my agent called. I took the call in the waiting room.

"*The View* wants to talk to you again," my agent said.

I rolled my eyes. I'd guest-hosted in 2008 and in 2010. At many points since then, it felt like they'd been on the verge of offering me a full-time job, but they never had. I always was the bridesmaid, never the bride. They would say: "You can be our rotating guest host every three weeks!" And I would say: "No way. I'm nobody's fourth choice."

But now, my agent said, they wanted to talk again. Now, when I only wanted to be around my father and help him to get through his cancer treatment. Great timing, guys.

"No," I told my agent. "They're too late. I'm not interested. I want to help my dad now. I don't have the bandwidth for a new job, and also, *no way.* I feel like daytime TV these days is all cooking segments, DIY decorative makeovers, and stuff about being a mom. It's insulting."

When I hung up, I saw my father staring at me from his adjoining seat. He'd been listening in on my side of the call and thought I'd just made a huge mistake. He told me how much he'd enjoyed watching me on Fox and that I had a gift for TV that shouldn't go to waste. He said on *The View*, I would enjoy spending time with Whoopi. They'd done work together over the years on Capitol Hill, and it had led to a warm friendship.

I pushed back. To me, it seemed that *The View* was on its last legs. They'd been bleeding an audience to CBS's *The Talk*. To win people back, the producers appeared to be trying to make the show lighter and more about pop culture. If I were on there, I'd insist on treating our audience as if the show was less *Entertainment Tonight* and more *This Week with George Stephanopoulos*. I thought they needed to dial down the Hollywood gossip and bring on more political heavyweights. How would that fly?

My father seemed unconvinced by my tirade. He told me to call back and say I'd take the job.

"The show is bad!" I told him. "They're always talking about celebrities and yelling at each other. Plus, they have a huge turnover rate. No one survives more than a season."

Every time I turned it on, they were talking about the Kardashians. I wanted no part of trashy conversations. I was disappointed in the show for not giving the women of America more credit. What I saw in the culture was women on the Right and the Left who were more politically engaged than ever, and no outlet talking to them seriously about the issues of the day.

"Yes! That's right!" my father said. "That's why they need *you*!"

He picked up my phone and dialed my agent, and then handed me back the ringing phone with the words: "Just tell him you're interested."

When my agent picked up, I said, "Hey, so my dad made me call you back. He says that you have to go back to ABC and say I'm interested. I'm here with him at his cancer treatment, so I guess I have to do whatever he wants."

I looked over at my father. He smiled and nodded.

"What do you want to take the gig?" my agent asked.

"I want X amount of money," I said, naming my ideal salary. "And I want them to make a formal offer today. And that's it. If they act the way they have in the past and drag this out for weeks, the end. *No mas!*" My father used that phrase all the time. It's what the boxer Roberto Durán said after eight rounds in the ring with Sugar Ray Leonard to signal that he'd had enough.

To ABC's credit, they met both of my demands. By the time my father and I got back home that evening after our day at the hospital, I had been hired by *The View*.

I started a few weeks later, in October. I was torn about having to be in New York so much when my dad was sick in Arizona, but ABC surprised me there, too. They let me take every other Friday off so I could fly to see my dad and help him with his treatment. They gave me a soft cushion to reenter the workforce at a hard time. I started to think that I was very lucky to have taken my father's advice, especially because it made him happy to see me flourishing. Whenever I felt guilty that I was back at work instead of with him, he said, "What are we going to do—just sit around and stare at each other all day?"

Then the nasty headlines began.

"EXCLUSIVE: 'They've nicknamed her Elsa from *Frozen*!' Meghan McCain's 'cold and distant demeanor' is causing tension among her co-hosts on *The View* after she snubbed Sunny and Sara [Haines] on air but was 'brown-nosing' Whoopi."

"*The View*'s Joy Behar threatens to quit over 'entitled b*tch' Meghan McCain—who staffers mock as the 'ice princess.'"

Scrolling through them, I thought, *I guess this is the big leagues?* I was also mad that no one was talking about anything I'd done on-air. All the stories were about how I was supposedly cold behind the scenes, implying that it was unacceptable to be treating my job as a job rather than as a social call.

Joining *The View* was a hazing experience. I was shocked and very upset by the coverage, much of which seemed like blown-out-of-proportion gossip spread by someone who'd seen me backstage keeping myself a little bit aloof. To be fair, I'm sure I wasn't the best company back then. My father was dying, and I was working very hard to do a good job. I was focused when it came to the work at hand but otherwise sad and distracted.

The news items always had a kernel of truth, but everything else was completely made up. For example, it might be true that I had disagreements with someone backstage, but it was not true that we hit each other or broke a mirror or screamed and cursed. I always joked that the leakers made me sound like Axl Rose on tour circa *Appetite for Destruction*, practically spraying gas all over the hallways and flicking matches.

I went to the executive producers and to the head of talent with printouts of the stories and said, "What's going on here? I am not here to be everyone's friend. I am here to help make this show better. That's why you hired me, isn't it?"

Talk-show environments tend to be hyper-social. That's not my way. When I came onto the staff at *The View*, I was assured that our set was a professional workplace and that I wasn't expected to bake everyone brownies. I was polite, but I didn't have a lot of bandwidth when I was trying to work very hard to research every topic and ask tough questions. I was flying back and forth to Arizona every other weekend. In between, I was distracted by calls home to see how everything was going. It was never good news. I'm also an introvert in my private life. I like to keep my circle small.

As I saw it, at work, I was there to get the topics in the right place and help book guests, and to try every minute I was on TV to say something compelling. It was hard enough without the pressure to be Miss Congeniality even when I was in my own dressing room.

When I first got there, the hosts batted around Hot Topics while we were getting our hair and makeup done in the room with the rest of the crew. In these meetings, it was my job to push for my ideas. I had been hired to bring a more conservative voice to the show. There were millions of women out there in the country who weren't New York City liberals, and I'd been hired to speak for them. And yet, in those first Hot Topics meetings, I met with a lot of resistance.

What I kept hearing was that I had a choice about what to cover. This was true, except these were the choices: (1) Republicans are evil. (2) Republicans are Nazis. (3) Trump will end the world. (4) Republicans want people to die. Those were basically the options I had to pick from each morning. I'm obviously exaggerating for dramatic effect, but it's not too far off.

At times it was a struggle to get even one pro-Republican topic onto the agenda unless I turned blue arguing for it. Then I'd read online mere hours later about my "meltdown" backstage.

Think of all the famously combative male TV anchors on shows with far smaller ratings and much lower profiles: if they raise their voices, they're respected as passionate and serious. If I push for my ideas, I'm a princess menacing everyone with snow monsters. The words for men behaving the way I did: *principled, ardent, powerful.* For me? *Shrill, maniac, meltdown.*

Chris Cuomo can bring out a giant prop of a nose swab. He can talk to his brother about their mom. The *Pod Save America* guys can yell all day long. But if Joy and I get in an informed, heated argument about socialism, suddenly I need a straitjacket.

The news articles all said Joy and I hated each other. It was true that we bickered, and that we disagreed on a lot of political issues. But from the beginning, I always respected her. And she often hugged me and told me she was glad I was there. Her party line was: "It's like being in a band. Do we fight? Of course!"

Good bands fight because they care about the music. She and I both love the country, and we both have strong feelings about what it needs right now. I think it's healthy to model that kind of civilized disagreement on TV.

The constant media slams were so emotionally and mentally taxing that I thought about leaving many times during those first months. The only thing that kept me there was the lessons of my weird upbringing. My dad taught me I had to be tough and strong. He also told me that when you fall, you get back up. If you get hurt, you just keep going. Because of that, I refused to quit. Whenever some conversation from backstage leaked or some pundit wrote a story saying I was unhinged, I thought, *If you think that this is going to break me, it won't, because I can't let you win.* I accepted that it would mean being hated by cool media people.

And yet, I hope it's clear that there was nothing fun about any of this. Imagine going into a high-stress environment, where the whole premise of the show is you don't get along, but somehow people are saying that without you, everyone would be happy. Every single time, you are the problem, the angry one, whereas everyone else is an angel from heaven.

As a result, I became more private and more insulated, and so the things they'd said became a self-fulfilling prophecy. The colder they said I was, the more I withdrew, and the more I withdrew, the colder they said I was, and on and on, like a snake eating its own tail.

A while back, I heard a rumor about one of my bosses who has since been fired. People told me that she'd planted stories in the press about me and about other hosts who preceded me. The idea seemed to be that *The View* desk should be seen as a rotating carousel and that if you don't play the game the way they want you to, you're disposable.

Now, again, I do have perspective on this. It's a fancy job, and I'm lucky to have had this opportunity. The stress of being maligned in the press every day is objectively nowhere near as bad as it would be at a lot of jobs, especially ones that are exhausting but don't pay a living wage. I know that plenty is way harder than talking about politics in front of a camera. And yet, the environment at *The View* has at times been toxic, and it certainly took its toll on me.

I've gone back and forth about whether to even talk about this, but I think part of the problem is too many people haven't talked about it, which is why this environment has continued to exist. I have discussed this problem with executives at ABC, so it shouldn't come as a shock to them that I feel this way. The show has been on for almost twenty-five years. With that comes twenty-five years of bad habits.

In fairness, many of the twenty-two hosts to date didn't last very long on the show. And I get that the producers would have something to gain from creating drama. But I don't respect that way of doing business. I think you should commit to talent and commit to people, and commit to shows, and recognize that TV is fickle, and all we can do is listen to our audience and do the best show for them. I think you hold an audience more closely doing that than creating this rapid turnover and getting people to tune in to see if this is the day that someone storms off the set forever.

Those scare tactics seem designed to make us, as hosts, go crazy, because it's good if we're going crazy on-air. If that's the case, though, they picked the wrong person with me. I don't think anything I've done or said or how I've lived is particularly special. But because of my father, I grew up understanding politics in a primal way. And he made me a fighter.

The network's evident strategy to keep me on my toes backfired because it turned out I worked as a host. A whole new group of people, especially a lot of women in the middle of the country whose interests had been ignored by the mainstream media, started watching. And they started talking about the show. Ratings are the main thing that matters to TV executives at the end of the day. It's a numbers game. And as I found my groove there, the ratings kept climbing, hitting their highest point ever in December 2020—number one in daytime television, including *Live with Kelly and Ryan* and *The Ellen DeGeneres Show*.

But if I thought the bad press would ease up, I was mistaken. The hazing in the media only got worse. The things that were written about me grew even more insane. I always heard about it the same way: a publicist would call me and say, "You're not going to like this . . ." Then they'd read me something from the next day's *Page Six*.

It got to the point where I was so worried someone would misconstrue something I said or blow it up into a big deal, I tried to limit my interactions and keep everything even more strictly business. On those weekends back in Arizona, I struggled to stay positive for my dad. He was going through so much himself, and especially because he'd pushed me to take the job, he was rooting for me to succeed. Neither one of us wanted to admit it, but I was miserable.

Still, the show's ratings kept going up and up. It was clear that I was part of drawing a new audience to the show, and I resolved to stop worrying about the bad press and to relish the incredible platform. I grew up watching *Crossfire*. It was one of my favorite shows when I was a teenager. With that in mind, I started to treat *The View* more and more like it was *Meet the Press*, the most serious political show on planet Earth. I worked hard and I did a ton of research for every segment. I was proud of helping maneuver the topics and helping us bring on more political people.

Instead of fluffy banter: "Let's have our coffee together, and how's your husband?" I would ask real questions: "Syria. You've said X in the past. Why?"

My goal is never to talk down to our audience. I believe that women who watch *The View* care about the details of politics. Even if they're stay-at-home moms, that doesn't mean they don't want to know about issues of the day. The audience is tremendously well educated and incredibly diverse—regionally, racially, and economically. My perspective on working on TV is that you should never dumb anything down and you should only ever punch up.

I didn't tell the producers what I was going to ask our political guests before we got out there, because I didn't want them to be overly prepared. And I didn't want our show to be seen as a cakewalk just because we were a women's show. I knew the producers wouldn't always love what I did, but I always prefer to ask forgiveness rather than permission. With *The View*, it has always been easier to do what I want and then ask later if it was okay.

The better things got on camera, the more liberated I felt. I realized backstage didn't matter. The press didn't matter. All that mattered was what I did on TV and what the audience thought about it. I started treating the table like it was my very own platform to reach women who cared about the country and wanted to hear things discussed in a way that acknowledged where they were coming from. And I could feel myself making a difference.

One and a half years into my time there, the *New York Times* put *The View* on the cover of its Sunday magazine, saying it was the most important political show in America.

This was the moment when, all of a sudden, everybody stopped questioning me. I noticed the press become less vicious. The producers decided I must have a method to my madness, and they started valuing me. To Whoopi's and Joy's and Sunny's credit, they seemed happy I was there. Even though Sunny and I are the most politically divergent on the show, we became close friends. It was never the hosts that were the issue. It was the backstage bullshit, and the media.

I was so glad I pushed through all that to get where I could make a difference in the culture. The thing that I'm most proud of in the entire time I've been on the show is getting the Women's

March defunded by the DNC in January 2019. Organizer Tamika Mallory was revealed on our show as a vicious anti-Semite. I asked her why she was praising Nation of Islam leader Louis Farrakhan. He's said countless horrific things about Judaism, including that it's responsible for "all of this filth and degenerate behavior that Hollywood is putting out" and that "Satanic Jews" have "infected the whole world with poison and deceit."

I pushed Mallory to condemn those remarks about Jewish people, and she wouldn't. I think all forms of bigotry are abhorrent, and I've noticed that anti-Semitism is a weird third rail that a lot of members of the media don't like to talk about. I don't understand it at all. But I was very pleased to see that the DNC removed itself from the March's list of sponsors right after the *View* episode aired.

I believe there is power in speaking to women in America. But there is retribution, too. We're still not in a place culturally where women can be seen and treated as equals in the media. That's why I still get actively and palpably jealous of people like Chris Hayes and Ryan Seacrest. They are always taken seriously in their spaces, no matter what. Meanwhile, we're leading daily hard-hitting conversations about culture and politics, and we're dismissed as gals catfighting.

The audience, though, is what makes it all worthwhile. Fans of *The View* project their personalities onto each of us, and everybody has a favorite. It's like we're archetypes in *Game of Thrones*, only instead of different houses, we are the tribe of the Blonde Republican, the Liberal from New York, the African American Actor. Each of us always has a gang of disciples in the audience. And it's a thrilling experience to hear that cheering and that booing. I don't need to jump out of planes because, every day, I get an adrenaline spike walking out there and playing to the crowd—those who are fans of mine and those who aren't.

A friend of mine was dating a woman who was an on-air personality, and when I asked how it was going, he said, "She's eccentric."

I said, "What do you expect? She's on TV. TV people were almost always the most eccentric person in their high school. This job takes a certain type of personality, one that requires outward validation—not necessarily a good thing. And I say that as someone who is like that."

Live TV is like walking a tightrope without a net. You can make an ass out of yourself, or it could be the greatest thing ever. I always think the camera's a weapon, and you can use it for good or evil. There is nothing in the world that I find more satisfying than the validation of creating something every day. I was a daily columnist on the *Daily Beast* forever ago, and a blogger on the campaign trail, and I got to love creating something and presenting it and then getting to do it over again the next day.

Every morning starts when you get the news briefs and start going over Hot Topics. The closer it gets to showtime, the higher my adrenaline climbs. But I like that—the challenge of getting just one shot with each guest. Regardless of whether or not the show goes well that day, I crash after. I'm so exhausted, I have to go home and nap.

When it comes time to interview our guests, I have forty seconds to get what I need to say out and to land a hit, pose a question, get us somewhere compelling. I've always found it rewarding because when I'm able to do it, there is nothing I'm prouder of. I never wanted someone to come on the show and get a totally free pass to say liberal talking points with no challenge. They should have to explain themselves. The strength in our show comes from the fact that we don't all agree on everything. I'm always ready to be surprised. And the guests certainly have obliged!

When the journalist Michael Wolff came on the show to discuss his book *Fire and Fury*, I mentioned that a number of people, including Maggie Haberman, Tony Blair, and Jonathan Martin, had called the book's credibility into question.

By way of defending himself, he mentioned a scene in the book about having dinner with Roger Ailes and Trump after the election but before the inauguration.

I was glad he brought that up because, when reading the book, I'd thought, *This sounds like something that would definitely have been off the record.*

I asked him about it, and he said it *had* been off the record, but then Ailes died. ("Not at the dinner," Whoopi quipped.)

That kind of maneuvering is one reason why a lot of people hate journalists. I felt that it was proper that he be put on the spot because I thought he'd abused his position of power and violated people's trust.

I can't be indecent to people or lie. But the producers and the head of ABC News give us a lot of runway to land on. And that freedom is a great part of the job.

James Comey was so slick and rehearsed that he was a terrible guest.

Rachel Maddow, same thing. I didn't get anything good out of her because she's too shrewd.

We had Donald Trump Jr. on for the five thousandth episode, and it was a disaster. He stacked the audience with Trump supporters, and he brought his girlfriend, Kimberly Guilfoyle, who I used to work with at Fox News (before she was fired for allegedly sending around penis pictures). It felt a lot like an episode of *The Jerry Springer Show* or an MMA cage match.

Interestingly, Whoopi, Joy, and Sunny were clearly not used to being in front of a politically hostile audience. They were put off by Don Jr. having control and being smart enough to pack the audience with MAGA people, who kept screaming over us.

There was a point in the interview that got caught on my mic where I grabbed Sunny and said, "This has to stop."

It wasn't my favorite morning, but as a rule, I love how when a guest walks onstage, you have no idea what you're going to get.

Dennis Quaid came on soon after he got engaged for the fourth time, to a woman thirty-nine years younger.

Jamie Lee Curtis is one of the most wonderful angel ladies. She came on the show not long after my dad died, and she was beyond lovely. I still text with her on occasion.

Terry Crews has always been an incredible guest.

Tyler Perry is lovely, smart, and so supportive. I was a fan of his work before he came on the show. But after I met him, I saw that he has this miraculous energy about him. It's gravitational.

Pamela Adlon is terrific. We still DM on Twitter.

And *then*, some people came on, and you want to say, "Get out of the house, please."

Case in point: Judge Jeanine Pirro.

She came on the show and told us we all had "Trump derangement syndrome," and when we pushed back, she became instantly enraged. During the commercial break, she said, "That went exactly how I fucking thought it would, you cocksuckers!"

On the way out at the end of the segment, she threw her microphone at me. It hit my chest. Backstage, she started screaming at Whoopi about how she'd done more for Black women than Whoopi ever had. Whoopi is normally very calm. The entire time I've worked there, I've seen her truly mad only twice. And I get why Pirro would set her off. I don't think you can tell a woman who grew up in the projects and became one of the most famous actresses in America—an EGOT winner!—that her contributions don't count as much as Judge Jeanine's.

Backstage, Pirro screamed at the producers, at the security guards, and everyone else. Again, the phrase she kept using was: "You cocksuckers!"

Who says "cocksucker," much less shouts it a thousand times? It's the dumbest word.

I heard Whoopi yelling back at her and telling her to get the hell out of the building, and I thought I heard some stuff getting knocked over.

Pirro went on Sean Hannity's show that night and recalled the episode as if she'd been an innocent victim and Whoopi were insane.

I yelled at my TV when I saw that. For the record: that is *not* what happened.

My mom called me that day and said, "I saw the show. Are you okay? That was so crazy! Did Judge Jeanine hurt you?"

On days like that, I think, *My job is insane.* I believe it is this that my father hoped for me when he made me call my agent back in that medical office waiting room: a job where I could be out in the world, and where every once in a while, someone like Judge Jeanine would behave so badly I'd fall out of my chair laughing. That time I spent in Arizona helping my father—he was helping me, too.

CHAPTER 4

FUCK CANCER

★ ★ ★

For most of the fourteen months between my father's initial cancer diagnosis and his death, I was working at my new job at *The View* and flying back and forth to help take care of him—often alongside Ben, who at that point was still my boyfriend. We were there to help my dad through the radiation, chemo, and endless scans, and my mom with the heavy burden she was carrying because she was there the entire time with no break.

I learned that when it comes to cancer, no one can predict the path or the outcome. When he was first diagnosed, the tumor was in his frontal lobe cortex. The doctors removed it and radiated it, and it wasn't supposed to grow back. But it grew back almost immediately.

We learned about the regrowth when we were on the thirteenth floor of the National Institutes of Health. When he had heard the news, he turned to me and said, "I knew it was a bad sign that we were going to the thirteenth floor."

I think people would be surprised to know how superstitious he was. He believed in signs and symbols. If he saw a black cat, he'd get uneasy.

"We're never coming to this floor again," I assured him. "And we'll figure this out." No doubt sounding truly deranged, I told the doctors they shouldn't give test results on the thirteenth floor.

I became committed to assuming control and making the cancer go away. I was obsessed with my father's diet. I bought him the healthiest, most organic greens and tried every recipe that's supposedly good for cancer patients. I did research online and fell into ridiculous rabbit holes—a healer in Brazil! A coffee colonic! Crystals! Holy water from Israel!

Of course, it was all a form of Kabuki theater—holding poses, acting out ritualized versions of normal activities, doing stylized movements of cleansing. With some things in life, it feels too difficult to bear, but you push through. I was pretending I had control, and I did not. I have been told in my grief counseling that's normal, which I should find more reassuring than I do.

My father was sent for physical therapy to try to mitigate the effects of his body breaking down. Struggling to do the exercises, he grew increasingly irritable with his physical therapist. To my father, the therapy felt pointless. His body was disintegrating so quickly, and the gains he was able to make in therapy were so minuscule.

Every time I came home for the weekend, he could do a little less. At first, his hand would shake when he was holding a pen. Then he started tripping more. Then he was losing his balance. Then he tried to grill us dinner, and he had a hard time holding the grill tongs.

It was brutal, slowly losing him, physically as well as mentally, every time I went home. I was always on edge, waiting to see the next shoe drop. I imagined the battle against this kind of cancer as a game of whack-a-mole. Every time you thought it was receding in one part of the body, it would show up in another.

Throughout the ordeal, my family was amazing. I always say we're an example of blended families done right because we love and respect one another. I have six siblings—we've got one up on the Brady Bunch. My dad was married before he met my mom. He and his first wife, Carol, had one daughter, Sidney, and he adopted his wife's two children, Andy and Doug. Then, after he got back from Vietnam, he and his first wife got divorced, and he met my mom. They got married very quickly, three months after they met. I was their first child together.

My siblings are all compelling people. My brother Doug is a pilot, and my brother Andy works for my mom's company in Arizona. My sister Sidney works in the music industry. The siblings that I grew up with were Jack, Jimmy, and Bridget. Jack recently got out of the Navy. Jimmy, who I'm the closest with, got out of the Marines, missed the military, and reenlisted in the Army. He's now living on a vineyard in Cornville, Arizona, with his family. He always did love fantasy, and he's always been irreverent. My sister Bridget is at Arizona State, becoming a speech therapist.

When my dad was sick, I was so grateful we all got along. In other families, I've seen tension between step- or half-siblings. But from the time when we were little, my father always said we were one family. When he was running for president, the media was always trying to get his first wife, Carol, to say nasty things about him, but she never would. They were good friends. When he was dying, we took turns taking care of him in shifts, and everyone had a different role. This is one thing that cancer sometimes does: brings a family together in a common purpose, strengthens bonds between people who already love one another.

But I can't think of much else in the way of good news.

My father had glioblastoma, multi-formed, stage four—a rare form of brain cancer, incredibly aggressive. What makes this kind of brain cancer so sinister is that it rapidly attacks everything that makes you the person you are. It's the same kind of cancer that killed Senator Ted Kennedy and Beau Biden, President Biden's son, and while I was writing this, Senator Evan Bayh's wife.

My father's doctor described it as "having glitter on your brain." And what you don't know is which piece of glitter will grow and spread the fastest. What key function will you lose first? What precious memory? It's crazy-making. As the doctor explained what would happen, I couldn't help feeling that my dad had pulled the worst card in the horrible deck of cancer. The average survival rate is a year to a year and a half, during which time everything is in decline. I became obsessed with stopping it from growing, and I imagined it as a lethal weed or strangling vines in a horror movie.

I wish I could say that my father's fight against cancer was inspiring and empowering, the way so much rhetoric around cancer tells you it should be, but the truth is that it was awful. It was a hor-rific experience, full stop. I wouldn't wish glioblastoma on my worst enemy. Every time I hear of someone getting this diagnosis, it takes the wind out of me. Every case is different, but every case is a form of evil. The journey is always arduous and painful. It took years off of my life watching my father go through it.

My father would do rounds of chemotherapy and radiation, and then he'd get scans to see whether the tumors were shrinking. They were not. A month after the original tumor was removed, it grew back. No matter what he did, they kept growing. He lost his mem-ory little by little—slowly, agonizingly.

I found myself thinking of that 1984 movie *The NeverEnding Story* in which the land of Fantasia is enveloped by "The Nothing." That was what it was like to watch my father forget his life—his rich, storied, love-filled life. I was watching the man I loved beyond reason be enveloped by darkness.

It was the last kind of cancer a man like him should have got-ten. Not that any cancer is good—they're all horrific. I cringe when I hear all the upbeat slogans around cancer:

"Not just surviving, thriving!"

"Cancer is a word, not a sentence."

"I hope, I fight, I win."

The only one I can fully get behind is #FuckCancer.

This one was the most cruel and inhumane disease anyone could ever imagine for my father. It went after the very things that were most important to his identity: his charm, his personality, his effervescence. All that was slowly taken away, little by little, making him weaker, flatter, and less himself by the day.

If I were diagnosed with it today, I think that I would take a bunch of money out of my bank account and take all my loved ones on a giant trip. And then I would probably go to the middle of nowhere and die quietly. I've seen the way people die of this disease. It is cruel and godless.

Birth and death have a lot in common. I thought labor would be beautiful and magical, with sparkles. But no. It was as intense as death. Watching my father die and my daughter be born both took a piece of me out of this world and into the next. I would never be the same after either experience.

People keep asking if I'm struggling with a newborn at home, and I am. I'll tell them that, yes, this is very hard, but taking care of my father was much harder. Every minute I spend nourishing my baby and waking up with her in the middle of the night, I know she's growing stronger and becoming more herself every day. But my father was fading away, so that kind of caregiving took more of a toll. I'm helping my daughter enter the world. I was helping my father leave it.

There's a viral video that people use all the time to make fun of me—it's a compilation of several dozen times I've said "my father" on TV. There's a cruelty to that supercut. Can't you dislike me without making fun of my love for my dead father? The video weaponizes my love for him and turns it into a punch line. If the point it's making is that I've been interviewed many times about my father— you got me there.

I've been on TV for the past fourteen years. My father was a famous person who meant a lot of things to a lot of people. I've been asked about him often, and I've always been honored to talk about him. My relationship with him is sacred, but because I have shared the sacredness of it, it's been used against me. Now I can't say those two words without feeling hesitation.

Everything about cancer involves surrendering control—something I'm not particularly good at. My father wasn't so great at it either. There was an HBO documentary made the last time in his life he let cameras around, *John McCain: For Whom the Bell Tolls* (2018). The crew came to the family ranch in Sedona (it's technically Cornville) when he was being treated. He talked in the film about being a "fighter": "I think there's no doubt that when I believe in something, that I'm really willing to fight for it." And yet, with this illness, he had to come to terms with the fact that there was no war left to wage.

My father was born on a Navy base in Panama. His father and grandfather were both Navy admirals. McCains have served in every American war since the Revolutionary War. My father earned the Purple Heart, the Bronze Star, the Legion of Merit, and the Distinguished Flying Cross.

But in the face of cancer, there was nothing he could do.

He and I both resisted the idea that cancer was necessarily "a fight." What if you have an extra-bad cancer and you get kicked on your ass immediately? And you're *trying*. You're not losing a fight. It takes you down because that's what it's designed to do. I understand that some people talk about facing up to cancer as showing strength, but I always preferred anger to strength when it came to this terrible disease. Some people don't want the quality of life that comes with the "fight" against the inevitable. Some people give up or decide not to seek treatment. I support everyone regardless of their choice. I think it's so personal, and it's so hard. And I support the way anybody does it. But it's just awful.

Those final weeks and days I found excruciating. They were hands down the worst of my entire life. The medical team seemed to not want to say anything definitive. Evidently, there was a belief that miracles do happen, and death comes when it comes, so it wasn't good to guess at timelines. But not knowing how long he had made me mentally unravel. For me, this idea that some angel was going to come down and restore his body back to the way it was, last minute, was, to me, not logical or helpful. And I wanted more data.

As a political analyst, I can always give a ballpark or a plausible scenario for an election. Even if I don't have definitive numbers, and I can be wrong sometimes, I can make a highly educated guess about any political situation. Why wouldn't anyone who knew about death do that when it came to how long my father had left?

Finally, two days before he died, I cornered one nurse and I said, "Please. I know you can't predict anything, but please give it to me straight. Stop bullshitting me because it's only making it worse. No one is saying this, but my brain is telling me that he's going to die very, very soon."

He was sleeping most of the day and only taking water via a rectangular sponge on a stick—it looked like a lollipop. These seemed to me to be clear signals that he was going to die soon, and I just wanted to hear a nurse or a doctor confirm it.

When I first heard that he was doing "palliative care," I didn't even know the difference between that and hospice. I had to google it to learn that palliative care is the doorway to hospice, which is the doorway to death. Looking back, I realize that I had no idea what to expect from any of it. Western culture does a good job of pretending death doesn't exist. Some Eastern cultures treat it as a natural process, but it feels almost taboo to discuss in this country.

The nurse tried to say that there was no telling how much longer it would be until he died, but I said, "Please, please tell me the truth. What's making this harder for me is this false hope. I'm not saying that to be disrespectful—I know you've been trained to say this—but please tell me how soon, because I need to start preparing myself as much as possible. Is it twenty-four hours? Forty-eight hours?"

"Very soon," she said. "The next few days."

I felt a flood of relief to at least know that much. I was also overcome with paralyzing fear. It was like being told I was about to get in a bad car accident.

"Thank you so much," I said. "For what it's worth, I don't think you broke the Hippocratic Oath or anything like that. I needed to hear it."

I found myself remembering a moment with my father from many years before. He and I were on a small plane together, going from one campaign stop to another. On the descent, there was terrible turbulence. We were tossed all over the sky. People on the plane started to freak out. I was growing nervous myself, not to mention a little bit airsick, but my father was calm as could be.

"Why aren't you worried?" I asked.

"Because I don't die in a plane."

As a pilot, he'd crashed before. It didn't kill him. He never worried on board a plane ever again.

"How do you die, then?" I asked.

"Surrounded by people I love," he said, "in Sedona."

And he was right.

Sedona was his sanctuary. Since buying this land many years before, he'd turned it from a desert wasteland into a place full of life, full of trees and grass, snakes and eagles and bats—he was always putting up more houses for the bats. He was so proud of what this piece of earth had become. He loved hosting his friends here, dancing along to music while he grilled food for everyone. So many of the most beautiful memories of my childhood took place here. When I was a little girl, he'd take me outside when it rained; we'd splash in the creek while he sang "Singin' in the Rain." We would hike in the hills and watch the hawks. This place was very much alive. And this was where he would die.

On August 25, 2018, I woke up and I shook Ben awake. I said I thought my father was going to die that day. It was the same day that Ted Kennedy had died nine years earlier. I said that it would be so like my dad to die on the same day as his friend.

Groggily, Ben said, "I don't think so. But who knows?"

To clear my head, I got up and went for a hike by myself. I was crying and scared and praying. When I got back, I sat down to eat potato soup for lunch. I was so nervous that the soup spoon kept shaking and hitting the bowl. My brother grabbed my hand to hold it still.

For days, I could not get my hands to stop shaking from anxious energy.

I told my mom, "I think he's going to die today." She said she thought so, too.

For the two evenings before, we'd stayed up most of the night with him in his bedroom, my entire family. We were all in our pajamas, sitting around, talking softly and listening to his playlist.

The experience of being with my family in that room all night, waiting for my dad to die, felt sacred and solemn, primal and tribal.

My parents' room in Sedona, where he lay in his hospital bed, had a sliding glass door. It was designed so that from bed, my dad could look out over the grass and the creek that he loved. Sitting there, huddled in the small room with my whole family for days on end, I had the feeling of being part of a tribe that had gathered in a cave, looking out into the forest.

My siblings were sitting on chairs or the floor on top of one another. I was lying on my parents' bed, on my stomach, close to my sister Bridget. I was trying to stay awake, but eventually, I fell asleep. I woke up and I saw that I was leaning on Bridget. Some people in the room were asleep; others were awake. Next to some were cocktails, and next to others was Red Bull. I don't drink much, and I made a point not to drink all that week, because I wanted to stay fully present until the very end.

For most of the night, I was crying softly, and my brothers were praying. My mom woke us up in the middle of the night, saying it might be time, but we kept watching his breathing and his chest kept moving up and down, slowly, painstakingly.

As the sun rose and the morning went on, people petered out and came back in, and no one knew what to do. We did that for two nights. It was a lot of waiting around to see. With every movement, every breath, I would think, *Is this the last one?*

I felt so unprepared for the experience of death. I wish people would talk about it more, because I was totally in the dark and kept ravenously googling what happens when you die. Western culture is so uncomfortable talking about it. I was so angry that I lived in a society where we'll talk about anything except loss and grieving and death.

Sitting around in what felt like a cave in the forest, quietly monitoring my father's labored breathing, felt very primitive. It was probably the most authentic human experience I'll ever have. I could imagine people doing the same thing thousands of years in the past and in the future.

My dad's former campaign manager Rick Davis was there with us. His wife, Karen, went on a hike the morning my dad died and saw a giant red dragonfly on a lily pad. She was so taken with it that she showed me a picture of it when she got back. She'd never seen one before, and this one landed right in front of her.

"It's weird," she said. "I googled what red dragonflies mean. Apparently in Japan, they're sacred symbols, and in some Native American cultures, they arrive to reassure us when we're grieving the death of a loved one." I took that very seriously because my father was always very superstitious and felt a strong connection to Navajo and Hopi cultures.

But when his death came later that day, it was not delicate like a dragonfly. It was more like a tsunami that knocked me off my feet. When my father died, I learned that even the most peaceful death in the world—which my father had, surrounded by family in a place he loved—is violent. This was my takeaway about dying: it's violent. It's a lot like giving birth. It's hard to come into this world, and it is hard to leave it.

We wheeled his hospital bed out onto the patio so he could be outside one last time. We all stood surrounding him.

The moment he started dying, I moaned—a primal wail. Everyone says you'll know when someone's dying, and it's true: you do. I'd heard before that there would be a death rattle, but you don't know what it sounds like until it happens. And when you hear it, you will never unhear it. Everyone else in my family was praying or crying peacefully, but I lost all my composure. When I saw his breathing stop, I started flailing around. I turned to Ben, hitting him and saying "No" over and over. I cried so hard that I started to vomit. Ben guided me to the end of the deck so I could crouch on all fours and throw up over the side. I felt like a feral animal. I was completely overcome. I couldn't calm down. I couldn't catch my breath.

One of the hospice nurses told me I was having a panic attack. He helped calm me down, and then he put my father's oxygen mask on me. It was taken off his dead body and put on my live one, which was awful, and yet the oxygen did feel good. Jimmy's wife, Holly, hugged me and told me it would be okay. She put one of her hands on my heart and her other hand on her own heart and said, "Breathe with me."

Once I had pulled myself together, I went through the sliding glass doors from the deck to my parents' bedroom and sat down on the bed. I looked up at the TV. An alert read, "Breaking news: John McCain has died." I thought how weird it was to experience a sacred moment and then to see it announced moments later on a news crawl. Evidently, one of his former aides who was there had informed the news stations minutes after it happened.

My father's body was mere feet away, still warm, but I noticed his ears turning blue. The coroner came. My father was loaded into a casket. Ben and my family members and I prepared to escort the hearse to Phoenix for the first of several ceremonies in two states. He was going to lie in state in Arizona, then at the Capitol, then in the National Cathedral, and then in Annapolis. For a full week, I would be following a dead body around. I wasn't sure I'd be able to make it.

Ben's sister Emily helped me pack up my clothes in the other room, and then we got into the SUV to leave. As we buckled our seat belts, Holly said, "Who wants a *road soda*?" Then she handed everyone a prickly-pear beer. Over the two-hour drive, we got drunk—sad drunk. If you've done that, you know how it feels. I am sure we were breaking the law drinking while riding, but the driver was sober. I hope the statute of limitations for us has expired.

On the drive, while we sipped our beer and cried, we looked out the car windows and saw people at what seemed to be every overpass from Sedona to Phoenix saluting our caravan, waving flags, and clapping for my father. I still don't understand how people knew that he was in that hearse or the route we were taking. But there they were along every highway, hanging over every overpass. The sight was beautiful and so sad.

We had to fly with his body in the casket on Air Force Two, from Phoenix to D.C. It's horrific to have to sit near a casket on a plane—distracting and uncomfortable. There were a million people on the plane. It reminded me of his campaign, only he was dead.

It was the worst plane ride of my life. What are you even allowed to talk about next to a casket? At one point, the plane turned because of turbulence; an older male family member who didn't have a seat belt on fell out of his seat and rolled down the aisle.

In the days that followed, I tried not to watch the news. It was too hard as it was, and I was so tired. But occasionally I would see something moving. A Native American man showed up outside the funeral home to perform a ceremony to protect his spirit.

After my father died, the guest list for the funeral leaked. No surprises: George W. Bush, Barack Obama, John Bolton, John Kelly, Jim Mattis . . . But another list also leaked: those who specifically were not invited. It did surprise people to see on that second, banned list, beside the Trumps, people like Steve Schmidt, Nicolle Wallace, John Weaver—and Sarah Palin.

I disagreed about Sarah Palin. I thought she should be there. She was still a big part of his life story, and she'd never been overtly disrespectful to him in any way. Other people around her had, but she hadn't. So, I didn't agree with that decision. But I was overruled.

There's always been a tension about who knew my father best, and it might be even more tense now that he's gone. His legacy is something a lot of people want a piece of. A group of people who used to work for him all think that they speak for him. Obviously, given that I share DNA with him, I think that I have some claim on one truth about him. But I understand that others feel that way, too. My dad made everybody feel as though they were singularly important to him.

He could charm anyone. And seeing other people give their versions of who he was proved difficult for me. People imprint onto him what they want him to have been. I get it. When people die, they sometimes become one-dimensional symbols. And everyone rewrites history. I saw people on TV saying, "I always loved him." And I'd yell at the TV, "You talked shit about him for *years*." I felt so protective of him and hated that, in death, people were jockeying for position, trying to assert their closeness to him when they weren't close to him at all.

When people told stories about him that rang false, it made me sad that they seemed to feel nostalgia for a person who never existed. This saint people make him out as is neither who he was nor who I would want him to be. People say how much they admired him when, in the next breath, they'd say something totally banal. It's wonderful he inspired so many people and that people admired him, but they are wrong to cast him as a perfect civil servant who never made any mistakes. I wish people would not turn him into something he wasn't.

"He was the ultimate statesman," former staffers said. "He always loved people."

Oh yeah? There's a bunch of footage of him yelling at people on the Senate floor. When he returned after his surgery to vote no in the repeal of Obamacare, he scolded his colleagues right after they'd given him a standing ovation welcoming him back.

"We're getting nothing done, my friends! We're getting nothing done."

He spoke off the cuff and refused to be censored, which is incredibly rare for a politician. He had the filthiest mouth. I loved that about him. It's probably why I swear so much, too. He's no

Romney. He was as wild as river rapids. And he was fun to watch. You never knew what was going to happen.

At the same time, he was a good protector. My childhood was so all-American that there's not a lot to say that would be interesting to anyone. I played softball and went to an all-girls Catholic school. I didn't get in trouble that much. Our parents kept us in a tightly controlled, safe environment.

One of the things I've come to discover as I've gotten older is that the way I was raised has had a profound effect on how I see the world. I have a deep respect for the military and for the flag, and I'm very deferential to authority. I made us start saying "Thank you for your service" whenever service members came on *The View*. At the same time, Ben calls me "a Western girl." I was raised to love the wild and to question everything. I have found traditional liberals to have a faith in government that I don't possess. I was raised to believe that we should never give lawmakers too much power over our lives.

Growing up, I was also made comfortable with guns from an early age. Everyone had guns and knew how to shoot them. The guy I carpooled with in high school had a gun rack on his truck. Once, I brought a New Yorker home with me to Sedona, and when she saw guns, she actually shook; she was so scared of them. I feel lucky that I grew up comfortable with guns and with the great outdoors.

Summers were a whirl of hiking and road trips and barbecues and sparklers. My parents always went over the top for the holidays. On the Fourth of July, we would have Slip 'N Slides and paintball games and go-karts. We would hike and fish and cook on the creek.

My dad loved the Fourth of July so much. He loved to eat, drink, and be social, and he really loved to have a good time. He often said the wrong thing and made jokes that offended people. But even when you disagreed with him, you knew he wasn't full of shit.

I would become annoyed when people would describe my father as "kind."

He wasn't just kind. He was rebellious and irreverent and snarky.

I struggle to hide my dismay when people say, "He was so noble."

"Yes," I say. "That was part of it. The other part of it was that he was intense and fun, and he didn't take himself so seriously. He wasn't boring or prudish, and he didn't like people who were."

He wanted everything to go fast. He loved boats, roller coasters, and deep-sea fishing. He was impulsive, maybe because he almost died when he was younger. He hated feeling locked into situations or places. He was always living on the edge and doing things in his personal life and professional life to test boundaries.

He was a fan of *Curb Your Enthusiasm*. He loved Larry David's sense of humor.

He told dirty jokes a lot. Here's one I heard ten thousand times:

There were two guys in the middle of nowhere at a bar. One guy says to the other, "If you have nothing to do, I'm throwing a party later at my house." And then the second guy goes, "Okay." The first guy said, "There will be drinking. Is that okay?" And the second guy said, "Yes."

"Dancing. Okay with you?"

"Yes."

"Smoking. Cool?"

"Yes."

"There's going to be fucking involved, too. Is that okay?"

"That's okay."

"Great! Let's go! By the way, the party is just the two of us."

He loved chatting with me on FaceTime. Every minute of every day, he wanted to know what was going on.

My mom took care of everything money-wise, and he never paid attention to finances, so he had no concept of money, at all. He thought if he went to a five-star restaurant, it would cost $100. He thought cars cost $1,000. When he found out how much money I was making at Fox, which was considerable but not millions of dollars, not even half a million dollars, he said, "My *God*, Meghan!" He called my agent and congratulated him.

My agent said, "Uh, this isn't that big a deal. That's what a low-level Fox contributor gets now."

But my father told my agent he was being humble because: "That's a *lot*."

When I was little, my school hosted a Father's Day father-daughter hike. As a special treat to commemorate the day, we made tie-dyed T-shirts for our dads. All the dads opened the gifts and saw the shirts, said something grateful, and then set them down. But my dad immediately pulled off his shirt—chest hair in full view—and put on the tie-dye one.

"I love it!" he said and beamed.

The other dads saw him wearing it, and one by one, they put their tie-dye shirts on, too.

I was little, but I noticed that. I thought to myself, *He does things, and then other people do them.*

That pride in things I created was a reocurring theme. He always made an effort to show me how excited he was about anything I did. When I first started working at *Newsweek* when I was in college, I worked for a section called "Tip Sheet," which covered products and pop culture. It wasn't taken seriously compared to the rest of the sections of the magazine. I remember I did something on the season's lip glosses. He had my lip-gloss story framed and put in his office.

He liked shitty food—hot dogs and hamburgers and peanut butter and jelly. He didn't have the palate for anything high-end. He liked éclairs, and vodka straight. Belvedere Vodka over the rocks with little baby onions, and then for some reason, he switched to Absolut Elyx when he was dying. He liked weird drinks. When we announced our engagement, my father made Ben take a shot of some Yugoslavian alcohol that Ben said tasted like poison.

He was a terrible cook, except for a few dishes. We were always worried we were going to get salmonella because he was not concerned with food safety. We'd watch as he used the same tongs he'd used for the raw meat to serve us, and we'd look at each other, worried we were going to get sick, but not wanting to offend him by not eating it.

I will never forget the two busloads of Vietnamese Americans who came all the way from California to pay their respects after his death. Despite his years of brutal captivity in Hanoi, my father never lost his affection and respect for Vietnamese culture. He had that capaciousness of heart and generosity of spirit. When I was growing up, we would go eat every Sunday at a Vietnamese restaurant in Central Phoenix.

Because of the injuries he'd sustained while being held captive for more than five years in a Vietnamese prison, he couldn't raise his arms or bend his knee. That meant he couldn't ride a bike or pick me up over his head. And yet, he was a weirdly fantastic dancer.

There's a video of him at a fundraiser for the Apollo Theater where Jamie Foxx asked him to get onstage, and the two of them got very silly doing the Robot together. Jamie posted it on Instagram and said, "This is another reason why Senator John McCain is so loved . . . he made u feel like politics and being a cool human being lived separately . . . he shined on 'em that night."

He could laugh at himself. He was humble to the point that it was ridiculous. When he was dying, he thought no one would remember him. I had to tell him, "You changed the world, and you're one of the greatest American men who ever lived." He was not convinced.

He had strange, hard hands. My brothers called them "lobster claws."

He loved to swim in the ocean, and he loved to snorkel.

One time when we went on vacation, he used sunscreen for shampoo on his head, and we laughed about it for a million years because his hair was greasy and disgusting.

On road trips, he'd become a classic fifties father, turning around to shout, "I'm going to turn this car right around!"

Otherwise, he wasn't a big yeller. When I messed up, he was disappointed, but he maintained a great perspective on even the worst tragedies. He wasn't hysterical about anything.

He was short—barely 5'8".

He had a short temper, too. He was stubborn in his ways. He was impatient. He could be insensitive.

The rules he set for his children and for himself were simple: "Don't lie, cheat, or steal, and everything else is fair game." I think those are pretty good rules to live by.

He led with love.

CHAPTER 5

THE EULOGY

★ ★ ★

As the days passed after my father's death, I began to lose patience with hearing people on TV talk about him. I tried to ignore it, but I couldn't help feeling cynical. It was hard, especially, for me to see people who worked on his presidential campaign in the year 2000 speaking on his behalf. Whenever I saw someone listed as an "ex–John McCain staffer," I'd think, *Well, if that's the best chyron you've got in 2018, I guess I should pity you rather than object.*

And I tried to show them compassion. Figuring out what to say about someone who has died is challenging, even when you have had time to prepare. My dad had told me while he was sick that he'd chosen me to give his eulogy at the Washington National

Cathedral in D.C. I didn't know what the Washington Cathedral was when I agreed to do it.

If you haven't seen it, picture a giant Gothic church, three hundred feet tall. It's one of the largest churches in the country. It seats four thousand people. Until I saw the building, I didn't understand the gravity of his request.

It's difficult to write a eulogy when someone's still alive. I had to write it in those raw days right after his death. I knew that it had to be reverential but also that I wanted it to reflect who he truly was. Threading this needle felt difficult because I was an emotional wreck, furious that cancer had taken my dad and taken him so soon. I found myself yelling at his memory in a stream of consciousness: "You left me here and now I have to do this alone and it's awful and I hate you for getting cancer!"

I couldn't believe I would have to sort out those messy, private feelings in such a formal, public way. Through all of it, the rest of my family remained stoic and unemotional. I was a basket case. I'd had no luck hiding my feelings even at home. How would I do it in front of television cameras and thousands of people?

The answer is: I wouldn't. In every one of those pictures I've seen from the many ceremonies, I'm visibly emotional in every photo. There's one of me crying over his casket in which I look apoplectic while every one of my brothers and sisters and my mom remain composed and appropriate. It felt ridiculous that I was so emotional. I was sure people were making fun of me for being so over the top and dramatic, but I couldn't keep it in. Whatever was on my face was raw and real, and I hated that everyone saw it.

My father dying ripped me open. My life was split in half: before my dad died and after. Everything changed. I now believe I was experiencing post-traumatic stress, but at the time, I just felt like a caterpillar trapped in a chrysalis.

Ben tells me I'm quite different than when we met many years ago. The nucleus of who I am is the same, but I'm much more serious; I'm much more closed off. I don't socialize with people I don't want to see, for any reason. I don't make exceptions. I'm much more intentional about the choices I make in my life.

Unfortunately, in that weakened state, I went back on TV soon after his death, and I could not catch a break. The president was antagonizing us on Twitter. The press was running a nasty story about me approximately every two weeks. Someone wrote of the stories: "Why Is Watching Meghan McCain on 'The View' So Fun?": "McCain is always desperate to play the victim, but her martyrdom as a conservative white woman is exhausting. Why should we feel sorry for her?"

The pressure got to me. As a result, there are a lot of clips of me on TV responding intensely. Knowing what I know now, I should have taken time off from the show even if it meant giving up my job.

When the time came to give my eulogy at the Washington Cathedral, I knew I would probably cry and stumble as I had the entire week. When my name was announced, I approached the podium. When I walked by my dad's casket, I looked at him and thought: *Why did you make me do this? You couldn't have picked one of your calm kids? Maybe one of, I don't know, the soldiers? Why choose me, guaranteed to bawl?*

I climbed up the high stairs. They'd set up a big apple box for me so I could reach the microphone. Teetering on the crate in my high heels, I looked out and saw every famous person in politics that I could imagine, including Hillary Clinton and Bill Clinton and the Obamas.

I took a deep breath and looked down one more time at my dad's casket with a look that said: *You made me do this, and now you're going to help me through it.*

And he did. I shook the entire time, but once I started speaking, for those fifteen minutes, every word flowed right out of me with an undeniable energy. Every time I'd rehearsed it, I'd made a mistake, stumbled, wept. Except this time.

I barely remember giving the speech, but I've seen clips on You-Tube. My hands shook as I turned the pages. Looking at myself up there talking, I think, *I don't know who that person is.* Also: *She looks upset but strong.*

Judging by the comments, people either loved that I was so angry and emotional, or they hated it. Some people thought it was inappropriate and not the way you should give a eulogy. Then there were a bunch of people who thought it was just right.

Ben deserves a lot of the credit for the speech itself. So many speechwriters offered to help me write the eulogy, but I felt like it was too personal, so I asked Ben to work on it with me. I loved what he wrote, and when he offered to help me practice it, I felt blessed.

Who else on the planet could help me through this? I thought.

Ben is a former speechwriter for John Cornyn and Tommy Thompson, and he worked in the speechwriting office in George W. Bush's White House. I performed the speech for Ben at least fifty times, many of them in my pajamas, as he gave me advice about how to use my voice and on the cadence of various words. I felt like I had hired someone brilliant—and very sexy—to work with me 24/7.

Right up until the day of the service, we'd been struggling with one line: "The America of John McCain never had to be made great again, because it was always great." I couldn't decide if I should keep it or not.

At the last minute, I chose to say it, because the last thing my dad told me about the eulogy before he died was, "Give them hell."

As the line approached, I thought: *This is it. Deliver it solid.* After I'd said it, I looked out, and the entire audience seemed shocked, except Hillary Clinton, who was smiling broadly.

I saw Ivanka Trump and Jared Kushner sitting toward the back. As far as I knew, they had not been invited by the family, but they showed up anyway—funeral crashers. It never even crossed my mind that they would come. Why would you go to something like that? It seemed audacious even for them. When I saw them, I thought, *I hope this is the most uncomfortable moment of your entire life.*

Then there was a pause, and suddenly everyone started clapping, which I was told later was the first time anyone could remember hearing applause at the National Cathedral during a funeral. The sound was cathartic. Thousands of people felt how I felt. I wasn't alone.

As I walked back to my pew after delivering the eulogy, everyone was quiet. No one was looking at me. After I sat down, my most eccentric uncle turned around and said two words: "Very good."

"Are you sure?" I whispered back.

"Yes," he said.

After the ceremony was over, I got into the van to leave and fell asleep against the window. When I got back to the hotel, I lay down in the bed and passed out immediately. I slept for ten hours. I was completely drained and blown out in every way.

I've often thought that I still don't know why my dad made me do that. It was a huge honor, but petrifying. Many people were surprised that it wasn't one of my brothers who was asked to speak on behalf of the family. But my brothers aren't as public as I am. No disrespect to them—they aren't built for public speaking.

I think perhaps my father also wanted someone to have the last word, and we were so close that he knew I'd say something he'd like. I think he wanted people to know how he was as a man and as a father.

Famous men often have strained relationships with their families. Fame casts a shadow. When I read the damning things Mayor Giuliani's daughter had written about her father, for example, I know of how rare it is to loom large on the world stage and also to be there for your family. But my father was that rare kind of man. Without missing a beat, he would switch his attention back and forth from his constituents to his children. I think he was proud that his kids loved him so much and that we ended up, by and large, pretty well adjusted.

Eulogies are now what I'm asked about more than anything else except life at *The View*. It's hard to know what to say, but I do believe that the key to a good eulogy is passion and true connection to the subject. I believe there's an advantage, too, in being raw and uncensored.

Looking back, I don't regret being as emotionally vulnerable as I was when I gave my father's eulogy. At the time, I was embarrassed. But now I think that if I looked destroyed, it's because I was destroyed. I was still in shock. I hadn't yet processed anything. And I was still so sad and so angry that he had died at a time when I felt I needed his guidance more than ever.

I will never entirely understand why he chose me to speak at the National Cathedral. And yet, I've come to see it as the most significant moment in my life aside from giving birth. A part of me died with him. Now that he's gone, everything is a bit darker; lights shine less brightly. I'm not the same person.

I decided to open the eulogy with a quote from his favorite novelist, Ernest Hemingway, whose books my father read to me when I was young: "The world is a fine place and worth the fighting for, and I hate very much to leave it." I continued:

> When Ernest Hemingway's Robert Jordan, at the close of *For Whom the Bell Tolls*, lies wounded and waiting for his last fight, these are among his final thoughts.
>
> My father had every reason to think the world was an awful place. My father had every reason to think the world was *not* worth fighting for. My father had every reason to think the world was worth leaving. He did not think any of those things. Like the hero of his favorite book, John McCain took the opposite view: *You had to have a lot of luck to have had such a good life.*
>
> I am here before you today saying the words I have never wanted to say, giving the speech I have never wanted

to give. Feeling the loss I have never wanted to feel. My father is gone.

John Sidney McCain III was many things. He was a sailor, he was an aviator, he was a husband, he was a warrior, he was a prisoner, he was a hero, he was a congressman, he was a senator, he was a nominee for president of the United States. These are all the titles and the roles of a life that has been well lived. They are not the greatest of his titles nor the most important of his roles.

He was a *great* man. We gather here to mourn the passing of American greatness, the real thing, not cheap rhetoric from men who will never come near the sacrifice he gave so willingly, nor the opportunistic appropriation of those who live lives of comfort and privilege while he suffered and served.

He was a great fire who burned bright.

In the past few days, my family and I have heard from so many of those Americans who stood in the warmth and light of his fire and found it illuminated what is best about them. We are grateful to them because they're grateful to him. A few have resented that fire for that light it cast upon them, for the truth it revealed about *their* character, but my father never cared what they thought, and even that small number still have the opportunity as long as they draw breath to live up to the example of John McCain.

My father was a great man. He was a great warrior. He was a great American. I admired him for all of these things, but I love him because he was a great father. My father knew what it was like to grow up in the shadow of greatness; he did just as his father had done before him. He was the son of a great admiral who was also the son of a great admiral. And when it came time for the third John Sidney McCain to become a man, he had no choice but in his own eyes to walk in those exact same paths. He had to become a sailor. He had to go to war. He had to have his shot at becoming a great admiral as they also had done.

The paths of his father and grandfather led my father directly to the harrowing hell of the Hanoi Hilton. This is the public legend that is John McCain. This is where all of the biographies, the campaign literature, and public remembrances say he showed his character, his patriotism, his faith, and his endurance in the worst of possible circumstances. This is where we learned who John McCain truly was. And all of that is very true except for the last part.

Today I want to share with you where I found out who John McCain truly was. It wasn't in the Hanoi Hilton. It wasn't in the cockpit of a fast and lethal fighter jet. It wasn't on the high seas or on the campaign trail. John McCain was in all of those places, but the best of him was somewhere else. The best of John McCain—the greatest of his titles and the most important of his roles—was as a father.

Imagine the warrior, the knight of the skies, gently carrying his little girl to bed. Imagine the dashing aviator who took his aircraft hurtling off pitching decks in the South China Seas kissing a hurt when I fell and skinned my knee. Imagine the distinguished statesman who counseled presidents and the powerful singing with his little girl in Oak Creek during a rainstorm to "Singin' in the Rain." Imagine the senator, the fierce conscience of the nation's best self, taking his fourteen-year-old daughter out of school because he believed that I would learn more about America at the town halls he held across the country. Imagine the elderly veteran of war and government, whose wisdom and courage were sought by the most distinguished men of our time, with his eyes shining with happiness as he gave his blessing for his grown daughter's marriage.

You all have to imagine that. I don't have to because I lived it all. I know who he was. I know what defined him. I got to see it every single day of my blessed life.

John McCain was not defined by prison, by the Navy, by the Senate, by the Republican Party, or by any single one of the deeds in his absolutely extraordinary life. John McCain was defined by love.

Several of you out there in the pews who crossed swords with him or found yourselves on the receiving end of his famous temper or were at a cross purpose to him on nearly anything are right at this moment doing your best to stay stone-faced. Don't. You know full well that if John McCain were in your shoes here today, he would be using some salty word he learned in the Navy while my mother jabbed him in the arm in embarrassment. He would look back at her and grumble and maybe stop talking, but he would keep grinning. She was the only one who could do that.

On their first date, when he still did not know what sort of woman she was, he recited a Robert Service poem to her called "The Cremation of Sam McGee," about an Alaskan prospector who welcomes his cremation as the only way to get warm in the icy north. "There are strange things done in the midnight sun by the men who moil for gold. The arctic trails have their secret tales that would make your blood run cold."

He had learned it in Hanoi. A prisoner in the next cell had rapped it out in code over and over again during the long years of captivity. My father figured that if Cindy Lou Hensley would sit through that, and appreciate the dark humor that had seen him through so many years of imprisonment, she just might sit through a lifetime with him as well. And she did.

John McCain was defined by love. This love of my father for my mother was the most fierce and lasting of them all, Mom. Let me tell you what love meant to John McCain and to me.

His love was the love of a father who mentors as much as he comforts. He was endlessly present for us. And though we did not always understand it, he was always teaching. He didn't expect us to be like him. His ambition for us, unmoored from any worldly achievement, was to be better than him, armed with his wisdom and informed by his experiences, long before we were even old enough to have assembled our own.

As a girl I didn't fully appreciate what I most fully appreciate now: how he suffered and how he bore it with a stoic silence that was once the mark of an American man.

I came to appreciate it first when he demanded it of me. I was a small girl, thrown from a horse and crying from a busted collarbone. My dad picked me up. He took me to the doctor, and he got me all fixed up. Then he immediately took me back home and made me get back on that very same horse. I was furious at him as a child, but how I love him for it now.

My father knew pain and suffering with an intimacy and immediacy that most of us are blessed never to have endured. He was shot down, he was crippled, he was beaten, he was starved, he was tortured, and he was humiliated. That pain never left him. The cruelty of his communist captors ensured that he would never raise his arms above his head for the rest of his life. Yet he survived. Yet he endured. Yet he triumphed. And there was this man who had been through all that with a little girl who simply didn't want to get back on her horse.

He could have sat me down and told me all of that and made me feel small because my complaint and my fear was nothing next to his pain and memory. Instead, he made me feel loved. "Meghan," he said in his quiet voice that spoke with authority and meant you had best obey. "Get back on the horse." I did. And because I was a little girl, I resented it. Now that I am a woman, I look back across that time and see the expression on his face when I climbed back up and rode again, and I see the pride and love in his eyes as he said, "Nothing is going to break you."

For the rest of my life, whenever I fall down, I get back up. Whenever I am hurt, I drive on. Whenever I am brought low, I rise. That is not because I am uniquely virtuous or strong or resilient; it is simply because my father, John McCain, was.

When my father got sick, when I asked him what he wanted me to do with this eulogy, he said, "Show them how tough you are." That is what love meant to John McCain.

Love for my father also meant caring for the nation entrusted to him. My father, the true son of his father and grandfather, was born into an enduring sense of the hard-won character of American greatness, and was convinced of the need to defend it with ferocity and faith. John McCain was born in a distant and now vanquished outpost of American power, and he understood America as a sacred trust. He understood our republic demands responsibilities, even before it defends its rights. He knew navigating the line between good and evil was often difficult but always simple. He grasped that our purpose and our meaning was rooted in a missionary's responsibility, stretching back centuries.

Just as the first Americans looked upon a new world full of potential for a grand experiment in freedom and self-government, so their descendants have a responsibility to defend the old world from its worst self. The America of John McCain is the America of the revolution, fighters with no stomach for the summer soldier and the sunshine patriot, making the world anew with the bells of liberty. The America of John McCain is the America of Abraham Lincoln, fulfilling the promise of the Declaration of Independence that all men are created equal, and suffering greatly to see it through. The America of John McCain is the America of the boys who rushed the colors in every war across three centuries, knowing that in them is the life of the republic, and particularly those by their daring, as Ronald Reagan said, gave up their chance at being husbands and fathers and grandfathers and gave up their chance to be revered old men. The America of John McCain is, yes, the America of Vietnam, fighting the fight, even in the most forlorn cause, even in the most grim circumstances, even in the most distant and hostile corner of the world, standing even in defeat for the life and liberty of other peoples in other lands.

The America of John McCain is generous and welcoming and bold. She is resourceful and confident and secure. She meets her responsibilities. She speaks quietly because she is strong. America does not boast because she has no need to. The America of John McCain has no need to be made great again because America was always great. That fervent faith, that proven devotion, that abiding love, that is what drove my father from the fiery skies above the Red River Delta to the brink of the presidency itself.

Love defined my father. As a young man he wondered if he would measure up to his distinguished lineage. I miss him so badly. I want to tell him that he did. But I take small comfort in this. Somewhere in the great beyond where the warriors go, there are two admirals of the United States meeting their much-loved son. They are telling him he is the greatest among them.

Dad, I love you. I always have. All that I am, all that I hope, all that I dream is grounded in what you taught me. You loved me and you showed me what love must be. An ancient Greek historian wrote that "the image of great men is woven into the stuff of other men's lives." Dad, your greatness is woven into my life, it is woven into my mother's life, it is woven into my sister's life, and it is woven into my brothers' lives. It is woven into the life and liberty of the country you sacrificed so much to defend.

Dad, I know you were not perfect. We live in an era where we knock down old American heroes for all their imperfections when no leader wants to admit to fault or failure. You were an exception and you gave us an ideal to strive for.

Look, I know you can see this gathering here in this cathedral. The nation is here to remember you. Like so many other heroes, you leave us draped in the flag you loved. You defended it, you sacrificed for it, you have always honored it. It is good to remember we are Americans. We don't put our heroes on pedestals just to remember them; we raise them up because we want to emulate their virtues. This is how we honor them, and this is how we will honor you.

My father is gone. My father is gone and my sorrow is immense, but I know his life, and I know it was great because it was good. And as much as I hate to see him go,

I do know how it ended. I know that on the afternoon of August 25th in front of Oak Creek in Cornville, Arizona, surrounded by the family he loved so much, an old man shook off the scars of battle one last time and arose a new man to pilot one last flight up and up and up, busting clouds left and right, straight on through to the kingdom of heaven. And he slipped the earthly bonds, put out his hand, and touched the face of God.

I love you, Dad.

CHAPTER 6

TRUE ROMANCE

When I was dating, I got the feeling that I emasculated a lot of men. I went out with guys who were threatened by a woman who was independent. I had my own job and my own life and didn't need to be supported or put on a pedestal, and a lot of men seemed not to know what to do with that.

And when I was single, I did a *lot* of dating. Oh, the bad dates I went on!

I hung out with so many guys who were straight who I was sure were gay and guys who were gay who I was sure were straight. I feel like I spent years staring across restaurant tables at men, thinking, *Do you want to just be my friend? Why do you keep taking me out to dinner?*

Over the years, I had plenty of bad breakups. I got ghosted. I got dumped. I had to disentangle myself from a raging alcoholic. But I was pretty good at shaking off the bad experiences. I always prided myself on being the best person to be broken up with because I had this line that would mess with guys' heads. I had always played the long game.

No matter how the breakup was worded, I would always say the same thing in response: "Thank you for the candor."

It doesn't make sense. It's not emotive.

More than once, guys would take a break from dumping me to say, "Wait! What does that mean?"

"Appreciate your candidness. Thank you. Now, we can move on."

One, confused, said, "Can we get breakfast to talk about it more?"

"No," I said. "Why would we?"

My thinking in that situation was: We're done. Transaction complete. I have plenty of friends. I don't need more friends. I was looking for a boyfriend, and that's not happening here, so I will be unfriending you on Instagram and unfollowing you on Twitter. We're not in each other's lives anymore. Next!

When guys sent me shitty texts, I would wonder who raised them, and my go-to response would be a fist-pump emoji, a beer emoji, and an American flag emoji.

Again, it doesn't make sense, and then they're stuck trying to figure out what it means while you've moved on.

I would never be rude or unkind, but the second you were those things to me, I figured it was on like Donkey Kong. You want to be crazy? I'll be crazy back. You want to be cavalier? I'll be more cavalier. Dating felt like game playing, and it exhausted me.

The other day, my niece was embroiled in an antagonizing text exchange with someone she was dating.

"Give me your phone," I said. "He's screwing with you. No more talking. You're done talking. He's being a dick to you. Now, be a dick back." I sent him my patented emoji cocktail.

The young man was confused and contrite and stopped the games he was playing. The emoji blow-off has a 100 percent success rate.

If a man came at me with a clearly made-up story like, "I can't go on a date with you tonight because my great-uncle's farm burned down," I would just send emojis back. Or I'd send the minimum number of words. "No worries" was one favorite. Another was "All good." If I was truly over it, I'd just do a single letter: "K."

In those circumstances, the less communication, the better. That was always my advice for myself, and still is for my single friends: Don't let them talk it out. Don't let them make excuses. If you're done, be done. When you realize you can't trust them with your emotions, you've got to remove your emotions from their reach.

I was seriously involved with a Green Beret who broke up with me via email when he was in Iraq. He said, "I can't do this anymore. I just can't." I took him at his word and I never replied—or talked to him ever again.

My agent had thought for a long time that I should write a book called *The United States of Dating*, but I was too embarrassed because, after dating a lot of strange and awful guys, I got to a point where I thought, *I need to take responsibility now for my taste. Why am I attracted to this kind of person?*

From then on, whenever someone started to seem crazy, I'd say, "Nope, that's crazy. I don't do crazy. Not anymore. *No mas.*" I'd tell someone acting weird: "I just don't do shady. I can't. It's too hard for me emotionally and I can't. Bye."

At the same time, as a rule, I would go out with anyone who asked me out. My thinking was: it takes balls to ask out a woman. I feel an obligation to reciprocate. As a result, I went on a date with everyone in the world, every man with whom there was the slightest possibility of love. I went out with waiters, with finance guys, whoever. I didn't care what they did or how much money they made or any of that. My theory was that dating was similar to gambling at the roulette table. You have to sit there long enough, because there's a certain point when you will hit the number where you've placed your chips. You just had to continue to sit at the table.

Another analogy I liked was that, in dating, you must be a shark—you need to keep moving or you'll die.

I actually did Tinder for a while. Everyone who recognized me from TV thought my account was fake. (My friend Clay Aiken was on Tinder, and he also got kicked off because the administrators thought his account was fake.) I was on Bumble, too. Swiping felt like playing a video game.

Now there are special dating sites for celebrities, and my friend showed me her Raya account the other day. The people who are on this app! Ryan Phillippe! Channing Tatum! It's amazing. I had a flicker of wishing I was single again just so I could get on that app.

I went out on so many dates, but honestly, I didn't care that it was taking a while to find a partner. I wasn't sure I even wanted to get married, which helped take the pressure off. I think women have a lot of pressure put on them by society to get married and have kids at a certain age and look a certain way. I think you have a lot more fun if you cast a wide net and you're open to a lot of different possibilities. I thought: *If I get married, fine. If I don't, fine. Life is awesome in lots of different ways.* That approach let me have fun.

Then I met Ben. Right away, he said, "I want to date you." And the second I started to wonder if he was having a good time, he said, "This is really fun." No shadiness. No mystery. No games.

When we got engaged, we decided not to announce it right away. My dad was dying, and my emotions were public enough already. But in one of our weekly work meetings, I mentioned that Ben and I were going to get married—and usweekly.com posted the news soon after. I was reminded yet again that the things said in the makeup room don't necessarily stay in the makeup room. I made a mental note that I couldn't say anything there that I didn't want to see in the gossip columns.

Once the news was out, I talked about it on the show. I said that Ben and I had been living together for a while and: "I want all the single girls out there to know that I don't consider this an achievement; it's just part of my life right now."

When I said that, I got a flood of positive feedback. So many viewers agreed with me. Often, when women get engaged and flaunt their engagement rings, the message they're sending is: "Look what I accomplished! I've checked off this box!"

Society already makes women feel bad. Why do we make them feel worse if they're not getting married? It's not like I achieved something. I was just dealt a good hand this time after a thousand bad ones. That's it.

My sister-in-law recently got divorced. I said, "If you want to find someone new, it's a numbers game. Just keep rolling the dice. And be open to possibility."

As I mentioned in my eulogy, on my parents' first date, my father recited a creepy poem to my mother called "The Cremation of Sam McGee." The poem is about a Tennessee man who froze to death while prospecting in the Arctic and asked his friend to burn his corpse. I don't recommend reciting murder poems early in a new relationship, but it worked out well for them. They were together for thirty-eight years, separated only by death.

My mother, then Cindy Lou Hensley, was very polite, very ladylike, so elegant I like to say that she sleeps in Chanel. She's the most proper southern belle, and very kind. People sometimes think she's cold because she's not overly emotive. She has the world's best poker face, but she's never sly or sneaky. She knows who she is. And, as a rule, she didn't enjoy poems about dead bodies. But she knew immediately that this wasn't just any silly poem about huskies and cremation. The poem meant something to my father.

My own love story, too, began in an unlikely way. It was New Year's Day. A friend and I were sitting on my couch, hungover. We were eating bagels and watching reruns of *Real Time with Bill Maher*.

One of the guests was a conservative identified as Ben Domenech, publisher of *The Federalist*.

"He's really hot and conservative," my friend said between bites of her bagel. "You should follow him on Twitter." Then she repeated his name four times to make sure I remembered it. When I didn't do anything, she took my phone, opened Twitter, and followed him.

Before she'd even put the phone back on the coffee table, he'd followed me back and sent me a DM that sounded distinctly like a date invite.

"Is this guy asking me out?" I said, showing my friend the message.

"Yeah, he is," she said.

I wrote him back and agreed to meet him for dinner.

So millennial, I know.

Our first date was at an Italian restaurant and a onetime speakeasy in the West Village of Manhattan called The Beatrice Inn.

I didn't take it seriously. Going into the night, I thought he was too conservative and too nerdy. When I was getting ready to go and meet him, I was on the phone with my best friend, Josh, who lives in Los Angeles, and I told him, with total certainty, as I applied my makeup: "There is no way this works out. We're just going to dinner, and it will be a story. Then we'll move on."

Then, as luck would have it, we had a terrific time at dinner and decided to go out again. And again. And again. For two and a half years.

I would have happily continued on that way forever. Ben had been married before, and it hadn't worked out. I'd never felt the need to get married. But then my father got sick, and we knew a ceremony would mean a lot to him.

Ben proposed to me at the Mayo Clinic after my dad was diagnosed and we saw his first scan. I was crying in the conference room. When the doctor left the room, I said to my father, "This is terrible! You won't be around for so many things! You're never going to see me get married!" He was called out of the room for another test, and Ben turned to me and said, "Yes, he will."

We had to plan the wedding in two months. Ben proposed in September, and we got married in November. It was a shotgun wedding, but I wasn't pregnant. I remember talking to the wedding planner, and he said, "What about this napkin holder?" And I said, "Nobody gives a shit about the napkin holders. I can't tell the difference myself. I trust you. Just make it look nice."

He did a beautiful job. The wedding was very rustic and made the most of the beauty of our family ranch in Sedona. We had poker tables and blackjack tables because a lot of people in my family love to gamble. It felt very Arizona.

There was some drama with my wedding dress. I had only two days to pick it. I went shopping with a friend who's a stylist, but I was not into it. I tried on one dress after the other, and they all looked awful on me. I had a hard time finding anything in my size. I was baffled by everything I'd heard about how much fun wedding-dress shopping was supposed to be. I hated it.

"This is such a pain in the ass, and nothing is fitting great," I told my friend.

Finally, we found something from Marchesa that fit and we agreed was pretty. But between the time I bought it and when I went back for the fitting, the Harvey Weinstein scandal broke. Marchesa is designed by Harvey Weinstein's then-wife, Georgina Chapman.

The fitting was awkward. Even though Georgina wasn't there, there was this elephant in the room that was the Weinstein horror show.

The woman pinning the dress on me said, "Is your fiancé a good man?"

"Yes," I said, but what I was thinking was, *Compared to your boss's husband, my fiancé is the goddamned pope.*

Once I'd finally gotten the dress tailored and ready to go, my publicist called and said, "You're not still going to wear the Marchesa dress, are you?"

"*She's* not a rapist!" I said. "Why would I punish her business because her husband is a monster? Besides, I love this dress and it was hard to find."

In my mind, I was thinking, *Could this event get more stressful?*

Then, of course, the wedding was just beautiful, and I'm so grateful for it.

My father was beaming as he walked me down the aisle. We didn't know it then, but that was the last time he could walk without help. He was ecstatic, but he hated anything saccharine or sentimental, so he cracked plenty of jokes that day. (It has been an issue in my relationship that I'm not super romantic. I forgot our anniversary this year.)

At the wedding, my father was supposed to give a toast, and in the course of the toast, he made a joke that included the line, "So, I guess I should get the divorce papers ready for you guys!"

It did not go over well. People were groaning. My in-laws winced.

Then he said, "There's a romantic song that I'd like to dedicate to Ben and Meghan. This is my favorite song, and it's all about love and commitment." The band then played the song. It was "Proud to Be an American."

I laughed. I don't think my in-laws loved it, but it was very my dad. That's the kind of random stuff I miss the most now.

The doctors had told us that if we wanted my father fully present at the wedding, we should get married by the end of November, and so we scheduled it for two days before Thanksgiving. At that time, I said, "That sure is fast—he seems fine. Why don't we just put it off until Christmas or New Year's?" But I was glad I was overruled because he ended up getting pretty physically sick right after the wedding and went downhill very quickly.

The wedding was beautiful and special, but it was also very sad, too, because we knew it would be the last time many people would see him, basically healthy and in that way. He seemed to know it, too, because he kept talking to Ben—who he liked, which could not be said of any other boyfriends before him. My father said to him, again and again, "Take care of Meghan."

Ben didn't tell me that until later, which is probably good because I would have been too sad. Ben has taken care of me. Even though I wasn't the most enthusiastic bride-to-be, I'm certainly happy to be married.

When we were first dating, everything with Ben was easy. That's my biggest piece of advice to women who ask me how to find a boyfriend: avoid games. With Ben, I was never sitting around wondering: *What is he thinking? Does he like me?* He told me he liked me. He was totally clear, from the first moment, about his feelings.

On our second date, I said, "Well, how many people are you dating?"

Ben said: "Just you. I just want to date you."

"Okay," I said. "That's a different vibe." He seemed like a grown-up. And I thought it was a good thing that he had been married twice before, once when he was very young. He's had a lot of time to get it right. He had to make a lot of mistakes, too. He's lived a lot, and learned a lot.

Ben is much more conservative than I am, and he's opened my eyes to a lot of different perspectives. His friends and colleagues are much more Trump-sympathetic than my colleagues and friends, and their opinion is nice to have. Even though I disagree with a lot of it, it's great to have this community and group helping me make sense of my country. I credit him with keeping me grounded and not letting me become trapped in the New York City/D.C. media bubble. His family is blue-collar. His brother is in the military. He grew up pretty poor. He had a very different childhood than I did. His family is very religious. He's kind. I don't want anyone to think, "Oh, it's a completely perfect marriage!" One truth about marriage is that no marriage is perfect. But I feel very supported and respected and loved. We're real partners. We're solid. I didn't know if I would like marriage, but I do like being married to *him*. I don't know that I could be married to anyone else.

Ben has always made love easy. I am incredibly proud of how strong our marriage is and how we have withstood so many critics and skeptics. That I've found such an incredible partner surprises me more than anything else in my life. It's something I never thought I would have.

The best part about being with him is that he doesn't want me to change anything about myself. He gives me freedom and lets me do what I want. And he helps me accomplish things that I want to accomplish. When we first got together, Ben told me that one thing he loved about me was that I worked so hard. At the time, I was hosting on Fox and doing three hours of radio every day. He believed that it was part of his role as my partner to help me do the work I wanted to do. I don't know of a husband who's more supportive.

When our relationship went public, many people in the industry were critical. I was told by one person after another that we were a ridiculous pairing. The *Weekly Standard*'s Jim Swift shared an old retweet of Ben's from years before we even met in which he'd said he didn't want to win a date with me. Someone called this "dumpster diving to mock recently engaged couples," an assessment I agreed with. One person after another insisted that he was going to cheat on me or break up with me, or that we were mismatched. It's not an exaggeration to say—and I do so with only the slightest bit of schadenfreude—that many of the people who were hypercritical of our marriage have since gotten divorced.

Looking back on the months my father was sick and the hard time after he died, I think of how much Ben had to rally as much as I did. He was by my side for all of it. I always say we could never break up for a lot of different reasons, but especially because of all that we've been through together. I love him and I'm attracted to him, and we have a child, but most of all, I feel that we are teammates. That's the way our marriage feels—as if we're on a team together. We understand each other's worlds, and lives, and careers, and we will do anything to help the other person fulfill their dreams.

Marriage has been a ride. Everything in our first two years of being together was undeniably *fun*. We would travel and do all the things you do when you're first falling in love with someone.

Then things got hard with my dad getting cancer. Since then, we've stayed at that level of intensity, but the rough times have made us that much closer.

The hardest part of marriage for me is releasing control and having to compromise. In so many situations, I feel that I like my way of doing something, but in order to maintain a relationship, I have to acknowledge that my way is not the only way.

People seem very confused by our relationship. Ben's website is very conservative, so I've heard people say of me, "She's married to that wingnut?"

Whatever. I'm very protective of our relationship, but I also have nothing to prove. It's just a relationship, full of grace and frustrations, joys and issues, like any other long-term relationship.

Throughout COVID, we've been cooped up together for months. It's hard to keep the romance alive when you see each other twenty-four hours a day, and when you know it's the other person's turn to take out the trash and *the trash is still there.*

There's a quote I love: "Adventure may hurt you, but monotony will kill you." Especially now with a baby, there are so many daily chores—clean the bottles, do the laundry, make the dinner, rinse, repeat. COVID has been a paradigm shift for everyone. I look at life as different seasons. Even though this is not a sexy season for me, our becoming parents together has created a totally new form of intimacy that's at least as valuable as being wild and crazy and free. I would like to put on makeup at some point again and not be dressed like a hobo, but for now, I appreciate the quiet closeness we're able to have when the baby is sleeping, and we lean over her crib to marvel at her.

Real life, I think it's safe to say, is nothing like what we see on shows like *The Bachelor*. We always have to interview *The Bachelor* people because it's ABC. I don't think it's an exaggeration to say that the show is about as anti-feminist and regressive as TV gets, and yet everybody I know watches it.

I like reality more than fairy tales, and I'm so grateful to be doing all of this with Ben. Ben is really different from me in some ways. He grew up in a religious home with conservative parents who attended an evangelical church in South Carolina and Mississippi, and yet somehow, he doesn't have a southern accent. He was a child prodigy in the political world. He worked on a healthcare policy and started college when he was sixteen. He worked in the White House when he was twenty-one.

I couldn't have invented Ben. There are so many things about him that only work for me, and things about me that I think only work for him. We're so much alike. We share everything from stubborn personalities to a dream of one day living on a ranch filled with horses.

I am a much better commentator because of him. Even though he's more conservative than me, he can tell me his perspective in a way that makes sense and informs my own. I probably would be a full-blown Never-Trumper without him. He grew up poor, and he understands the perspective of working-class Americans from the middle of the country who have been disenfranchised.

We had heated conversations about Trump's second impeachment. (I was all for it.) But the baseline of our relationship is that I don't editorialize what he says, and he doesn't editorialize what I say. I respect his point of view, and he respects mine. We will say,

"Well, I don't agree with that," but never in a way that's belittling or mocking. We both love talking about politics more than anything.

For me, politics is an incredibly fun game. I think of it in my head as I'm sure the way sports analysts think of football games, and Ben speaks my language. We both have these weird childhoods completely consumed with politics. Every relationship has times when you think, *Oh my God! How did I marry you? How are we together?* I can't imagine being with anyone else.

But even in our lowest moments, we have something to talk about because we have a shared interest. And whatever the topic, I always want to hear his opinion and talk about it. I'm lucky to have my favorite political analyst living in my house. Talking about politics with Ben, I remember why a fair fight about it is so much fun.

When my father asked Ben to take care of me at our wedding, I wonder if he saw all the ways that he would make good on that promise: rocking our daughter to sleep in his arms, cooking me food when I'm exhausted after a day at work, or talking to me for hours about NAFTA. Dreams do come true.

CHAPTER 7

FRIENDS FOREVER

When my father was dying, Fox News contributor Kat Timpf, a close girlfriend of mine, became my grief whisperer, my death spirit guide. Kat and I originally became friends at Fox because we seemed to be the only women who came to the studio without makeup on and wearing sweatpants. Everyone around us appeared camera-ready 24/7.

Several years ago, Kat's wonderful mother, Anne, got sick and was repeatedly misdiagnosed before she was finally found to have a rare disease called amyloidosis. Symptoms don't usually appear until the disease is advanced. The time from Anne's correct diagnosis to her death was just three weeks.

Kat's situation with her mom was arguably worse than mine with my dad because her mom died so quickly. She told me that when they were at the hospital, her mom was responding to email invitations saying, "I'm so sorry I will be unable to attend. By then, I'll be dead."

Since then, Kat has worked to call attention to the disease, and she's been incredibly wise about death.

As my father was dying, I kept asking Kat, over and over again, "What's it going to feel like when he dies? Is it going to feel like a sharp pain? Is it going to be scary? Is it going to be happy? Am I going to cry?" I was obsessed with figuring out what was coming at me and how I could prepare myself.

"You're in shock," she said after the diagnosis. "You're in survival mode. When he dies, it will be traumatic. It will feel like a car crash. You will need to go easy on yourself. Take time off if you can. It's like a physical wound—you need to heal."

She told me a story about how emotional she was when her mother was dying. One day, she was on a Greyhound bus from her home in Detroit to New York, where she was trying out to be a Fox contributor. Someone took her seat and wouldn't give it back. She completely freaked out and started screaming, "Get out of my seat! My mother is dying!" Then she dumped the entire contents of her purse onto the person.

When she told me the story, she said it without embarrassment. "When you're experiencing grief, becoming hyper-emotional is totally normal," she said.

She was so direct and so straightforward. I always feel better after speaking with her.

As the first anniversary of my father's death approached, she said, "Where are you going to be? What are you going to do?"

"Nothing special, because I'm going to be totally fine," I said. "I'm in a good place!"

"Bro, you're not going to be fine," Kat said. "Call me at three in the morning. Call me whenever."

And sure enough, I wasn't.

She just seems to know every answer to every problem, and she has a dark sense of humor about life that was incredibly cathartic for me.

Having good friends like that who were willing to keep it real helped me get through a rough couple of years.

One of my best friends is Clay Aiken, who was on *American Idol* years ago and who has been my plus-one for decades. Ben doesn't care for parties, so Clay always comes with me to everything. That is why there are approximately a thousand red-carpet and on-the-town photos of us together, including one in which we are wearing matching Best Friend necklaces.

These days, we aren't going out, but we still talk twelve times a day, and he's helping me with baby stuff, because he's been there. He has a son, Parker, who was born in 2008. Clay taught me about burping, bottle alignment, and what a WubbaNub is. If you don't know, a WubbaNub is a pacifier attached to a soft stuffed animal, and its inventor deserves the Nobel Peace Prize.

When I found out I was pregnant, before I had my miscarriage, I went to the gynecologist and made Clay come with me. I also dragged him to the doctor once for my mammogram when I thought I had breast cancer. (It ended up being fine, thank God.)

Clay attended every single funeral, which is real friendship, and he found ways to be helpful all that week.

When I rehearsed my eulogy in the National Cathedral, Clay coached me on the acoustics. Because he's a singer, he understood what the cavernous space did to voices and how to master it. He taught me how to raise my voice and lower it at different times to maximize its reach in a space that's notoriously hard to speak in. He gave strong, cohesive feedback, critiquing me without emotion. It was exactly what I needed.

Then, when my dad was buried in Annapolis, Clay uncomplainingly walked the long stretch from where the service was to the graveyard. It was August, and it was incredibly hot. I thought the walk from the chapel to the U.S. Naval Academy Cemetery would be short, so I stupidly wore five-inch Mary Jane heels.

Unfortunately, the walk to my father's burial plot overlooking the river was extremely long. It was up hills and down hills, past fountains and past horses. I walked the whole way, obviously, because what else are you going to do? And it wasn't like I was going to go barefoot at such a somber moment. By the time I got there, my feet had developed horrible blisters that had begun bleeding.

Everyone present was uncomfortable because of the long walk and the heat, and it overcame one of the prominent generals in attendance. He fainted and fell against Clay as they sat in the rows of graveside seats, onto his leg.

Soon after, someone asked Clay to help with something.

"I will when I get this general off my leg," he said.

"Having a general on your leg" became a running joke.

I was a mess that whole week, and not always very nice.

At one of the services, my dad's photographer for forever, David Hume Kennerly, tripped and fell in the balcony. He bumped into a bunch of people and knocked over a lantern. I looked up and shot him a look that said: "Pull your shit together. You're at a funeral."

Four-star general Jim Mattis, who was then the defense secretary, gave my father's children each a flag that had been draped over his coffin. As I've mentioned, I was emotionally apoplectic. When Mattis handed me the flag, I put my hands over his so he couldn't let go right away.

He said, "I'm so sorry."

I said, "Make sure you honor him."

I did not say it in a friendly way. I said it *angry*, because he was working for the Trump administration.

There was a pause as he looked at me as if he wasn't sure what I meant.

"You know what I'm saying," I said.

He looked me in the eyes and said, "I hear you."

I bore him no ill will. On a personal level, I admired him. He was the Warrior Monk, Mad Dog Mattis. But I felt like he'd made a deal with the devil working for Trump, and I had trouble seeing past it.

When I said that to him, my mother and Ben looked at me, taken aback. Mattis scares everyone, and they couldn't believe I'd just talked to him like I was his strict schoolteacher.

But I felt like I had to say it. I needed to purge my frustration that Trump had been so cruel toward my family, going so far as to refuse to lower the flag on the White House in my father's honor. I just ended up taking it out on Mattis because he was the administration figure who crossed my path at that exact moment.

The whole week I was on edge. What saved me from totally melting down were my friends.

I've mentioned Clay. My other best friend, Josh Rupley, a hair-dresser in West Hollywood, was also a rock during this time.

When my father was lying in state in Arizona and my family and I were in a back room, we spotted him on the video feed, filing past the casket with a friend of mine from high school, bawling.

My mom's cousin said, "Who's that?"

I said, "That's Josh."

Our cousin said, "That's not Josh."

I said, "It is Josh. You just don't recognize him because he's wearing a suit."

Josh usually wears ripped jeans, T-shirts, baseball caps, and his hair in various extreme colors.

My dad loved to have Josh cut his hair. One time after my dad had gotten very sick, Josh arrived at my father's bedside with purple hair. When my dad teased him about it, he said, "Watch out! Now that you're confined to bed, I can finally dye your hair purple like I've always wanted!"

Then he went on to give him the gentlest, most traditional hair-cut, and even cut his nose hair and ear hair. Josh spent every holiday with me since we met. Josh loved my dad. And my dad loved Josh, who he nicknamed "Hollywood."

When I finally got to see him after watching him on the live feed, I joked, "You were like Janet Jackson at Michael's funeral."

The night before the National Cathedral service, the fire alarm at the hotel we were staying in went off *three* times, starting at two in the morning, and woke everyone up. My entire family, and all the staff, all the people who were there, wound up standing in the hallway, trying to figure out how to turn the alarm off.

I saw my brother-in-law, and I said, "*What* is going on?"

He said, "I guess it's just time for us to be up right now."

I said, "That's not an acceptable answer."

After the third time it went off, I put my bathrobe on over my pajamas, and I went to the lobby and I yelled at the concierge: "Listen, I have to eulogize my dad tomorrow, figure it out." And it stopped.

My friend Josh didn't come out in the hall.

The next morning, I said, "Where *were* you?"

He said, "I was on the first floor. I figured if it was a real fire, I could just throw a chair through the window and jump out."

Again and again in the course of that terrible month, my friends found ways to distract me from my sadness. In tough times, you need to find joy wherever you can. We talked about the fire alarm and the fainting general for days. I love my friends.

CHAPTER 8

ON AND OFF CAMPUS

When he was just seventeen years old, in 2008, my little brother Jimmy deployed with the Marines to Iraq. I went to see Jimmy off to war. If that is something you have had to do for a loved one, then you know what it's like to look out over a sea of impossibly young-looking men and know some of them won't be coming home.

While Jimmy was overseas, the 2008 New Hampshire primary happened, and our father won. Jimmy was in the Iraqi desert digging a ditch when his platoon leader walked over and said: "Hey, McCain, your dad won. Keep digging."

Our father *loved* that story. That was the military he remembered.

As I was walking into my Columbia dorm building one day, a security guard called me over. He said he was surprised to see a student wearing a Marines sweatshirt with a globe and anchor on it. He showed me his Marines tattoo.

It wasn't the only time I felt like I had a different background from my classmates. At the time, ROTC wasn't allowed on the campus. Some of my classmates seemed to have a somewhat elitist attitude toward the military. (And yes, I know it's ironic for me to call someone else elitist.) You feel like you're above it all because you're going to an Ivy League school in the same class as Julia Stiles and Joseph Gordon-Levitt, and you feel like you can explain everything because you just took your first "lit hum" class.

I considered myself an independent at the time. I wasn't a fan of George W. Bush's because he and especially Karl Rove were horrible to my family. But I knew I wasn't like a lot of my classmates. They seemed so easily offended and so sensitive. I grew up roughhousing with my siblings, and I've never been a precious person, emotionally or physically.

And yet, no one was mean to me because I was more conservative. In fact, one girl who lived across the hall sent me a top-secret email to let me know that she was a big supporter of President Bush, but she didn't want to tell anyone.

I didn't see the identity-politics insanity until I started going to speak at other colleges about a decade ago. When you're doing the speaker circuit like I did, you have a baseline speech that you tweak for each place. My speech was about conservatism. I'd integrate current events to make it seem fresh and relevant. That lasted about twenty minutes, and then I'd talk with a moderator from the school for a half hour or so, and then there'd be questions from the audience.

I considered it a privilege to be asked to speak. I enjoyed the trips, and the more I did it, the better I got at making a connection with the audience. It was always nice to be in front of a crowd where people could ask whatever they wanted. It kept me on my toes. Plus, it gave me an excuse to go all over the country to people I might not have seen otherwise. I got to spend time in towns from Walla Walla, Washington, to Pueblo, Colorado. Students were usually friendly and generous, eager to give me a college T-shirt and a key chain and to show me around. There was a robust exchange of ideas. Even though there was often disagreement, there was respect, too. It felt to me the way politics did when I was growing up—fun.

My run as a college speech-giver came to a screeching halt in October 2012 at Reed College. I didn't know how liberal the school was. I hadn't heard of it before I received the invitation. I just assumed if someone's inviting you to speak, they want to hear what you have to say. I showed up ready to have a lively conversation like always.

I gave my usual talk in Vollum Lecture Hall, describing my career path and talking about the state of the media and the lack of real discourse among people with different points of view.

So far, so good.

Then came the question-and-answer session.

There was a question about fiscal issues. I said I favored a flat tax and believed in a balanced budget. The student said I was prioritizing money over "fundamental rights," like abortion.

I said I'd rather not talk about abortion, because it's the easiest way to get people fighting. The crowd was already riled up.

It went downhill from there.

I tried to keep my cool, but I got more and more flustered with each question. And as soon as I started to get upset, the students smelled blood in the water.

A girl stood up and said, "This is a comment, not a question. You're only here because of your dad."

I felt like I was some kind of effigy they were burning for sport. I became certain they hadn't even heard any of what I was saying because it didn't fit in with their worldview. When I leave my house or turn on the TV, I'm constantly inundated with people who disagree with me and who have different values and different perspectives. I tried to argue that even if they disagreed with people more conservative than they were, it might be good for them to know why others thought differently than they did. But the Reed students were having none of that.

The moderator announced that there was time for one last question. A young man said, "The fact remains that people listen to what you have to say by the nature of you being on television or being an influential blogger."

He then asked a complicated question about tax policy. I said I wasn't clear on what the question was. Another student jumped in to rephrase the question: "How do you reconcile being very influential in what you're saying and not being a tax expert with talking about taxes? How do you reconcile being an influential voice with not necessarily being fully informed or able to defend the things you talk about?"

The question was existential. In other words, if you don't know every obscure tax policy, you can't take a stance on taxes. Does that mean that if you don't know every MLB player's batting average, you can't have a favorite team?

"If you don't like what I'm saying, you can find someone else to listen to," I said, feeling utterly defeated.

With that, the talk was over. There was an awkward meet and greet. The only thing I remember about what was said there was that everyone kept going on and on about how Ezra Klein had just been to visit the college, and he was the greatest speaker of all time, a genius. I signed a few books and then left.

In the car on the way back, I called my agent and said it was a disaster and they didn't have to pay me if they didn't get what they wanted. Then I turned to the events person who'd invited me, and I asked him why they'd set me up like that.

"Don't invite people like me if your classmates aren't capable of receiving us," I said. "You shouldn't have people like me here if this isn't something you guys can handle. I don't know why I'm here."

On the plane ride back, I felt mad and I felt stupid, like an idiot and a fraud. I was also *sad*. I'd finally gotten to a place where I loved public speaking. And I knew a lot of college students had enjoyed my campus visits. They'd say so. We'd had debates, but we'd also had a good time.

The fact is, I wasn't rattled because the Reed students were liberal or even because they were hostile. I was shaken because it felt less like a stimulating give-and-take than it did a dunk tank.

And from what I've heard, since then, the problem has gotten worse.

On college campuses, there has been a growing fear of being shut down over perceived infractions. It doesn't feel safe anymore to offer up theories or to speak freely. To move in that world is to be eternally paranoid that you'll say something wrong and be cast out of society.

That level of tension and anxiety is nothing I want to expose myself to. I miss it, but I also only have so much bandwidth in my old age. It's not that I don't want to have conversations or healthy debates; I just don't want to be screamed at.

A lot of prominent comedians won't do colleges anymore either. Students are so politically correct that they don't laugh at anything. In a 2015 interview, Jerry Seinfeld said kids today are always throwing out words like "That's racist, that's sexist, that's prejudice." But "they don't even know what they're talking about." Chris Rock said he stopped playing colleges because "they're way too conservative. Not in their political views—not like they're voting Republican—but in their social views and their willingness not to offend anybody."

Every time I think this can't get worse, it does. And I don't know who to blame. I don't know if it's the schools, or the students, or the culture in general, but twenty years ago, you could have a respectful debate.

I don't know how we come back from this atmosphere. I don't think that speech and violence are the same thing, which is apparently a controversial opinion. These days on many campuses, looting a store isn't seen as violence, but incorrect speech is. One weird synergy between conservatives and old-school Democrats used to be that both hated censorship and were big free-speech advocates, and maybe there's room for us to come together now to try to reclaim intellectual life.

All I know is, until it happens, I will do my best to stay far away from college campuses. I just don't have the stomach for it. It's not that I'm a snowflake or someone who can't handle criticism. It's more: Why do you want to go somewhere where you've only been invited as part of a stunt? That's what it feels like when campus people invite conservatives into liberal environments.

The inviting group makes a huge PR to-do out of it. Then people freak out and sometimes get violent. When the Minutemen— the border patrollers who look for illegal immigrants—were invited to Columbia, students stormed the stage physically. Why would you want to put yourself in that situation? I give it up to people on both sides like John McWhorter and Ben Shapiro, who still go out there to colleges and let aggressive crowds yell at them and throw things at them. I don't have it in me.

CHAPTER 9

THE ONLINE MOB

All spring of 2020, during the very lonely second trimester of my pregnancy, Ben and I were inside because of the pandemic. Outside, the country seemed to be convulsing. Between the virus and the increasingly violent clashes between protesters and police and the ugly political rhetoric leading up to the election, it was a bleak time.

When things started getting warmer outside at the end of May, I finally began to feel a bit better. After seeing no one for months, Ben and I went to Virginia Beach during *The View*'s spring break to see a couple of friends. One of our travel companions was a good friend of mine from New York. He'd made a total transformation in the years I'd known him. Formerly a total player and partier, he'd become engaged to a woman with two children and turned into a doting family man. They were all so happy that I found being around them inspiring.

Even better: his wonderful fiancée was a hairstylist! I hadn't had my hair done in four months, and I had long gray roots. While she turned me back into a blonde and made me feel like a human being again, she told me how fun and amazing it was to be a mother. Her kids were smart and fun, a perfect advertisement for parenting. By the end of that trip, I felt truly excited and happy for the first time since March.

But anxiety lingered. Like all reasonable people, I was sickened by the video of George Floyd's murder. I supported the protests against police violence. But on our phones, Ben and I kept seeing videos of protests turning violent and looting, including near our apartment in New York. Calling what was going on "unacceptable," Mayor Bill de Blasio had put an 8:00 p.m. curfew into place, something I couldn't ever have imagined would come to New York City. And the governor called what was happening "a disgrace." But I couldn't see that either one was doing very much to support the peaceful protesters while also protecting innocent family-owned businesses like the ones I loved in Midtown.

More than two thousand people were arrested in a few days. A couple of police officers were also arrested for attacking protesters. Macy's in Herald Square was looted, as were a bunch of luxury stores in SoHo. Someone graffitied the George Washington statue in front of Federal Hall. Finally, there was rioting on 57th Street between Seventh and Eighth Avenues. I lived on 57th between Tenth and Eleventh. Tons of buildings in my neighborhood boarded up their windows to keep them from being smashed.

The more videos of it I saw, the more I felt like things were spinning out of control. It broke my heart.

I love New York. Aside from my three years in Los Angeles, I've lived there my entire adult life and all over, in the West Village, Midtown, Tribeca, in Greenwich Village near NYU, the Upper West Side. I consider it a spectacular city, and I was haunted by the thought that some of my favorite local places, including the bodega where I shopped, felt enough in danger that they were putting up plywood. I hated violence of any kind, and I thought there was no justification for what was happening.

On June 2, I tweeted: "My neighborhood in Manhattan is eviscerated and looks like a war zone. De Blasio and Cuomo are an utter disgrace. This is not America. Our leaders have abandoned us and continue to let great American cities burn to the ground and be destroyed. I never could have fathomed this."

A writer on Samantha Bee's show, *Full Frontal*, retweeted me and wrote, "Meghan, we live in the same building, and I just walked outside. It's fine."

Her snarky post got retweeted more than a *hundred thousand* times. It quickly became Dunk on Meghan Hour on Twitter. Thousands of people an hour were making fun of me as being a privileged white woman and as out of touch and as everything else you can think of. I don't understand how people can ask for tolerance and unity when you get pleasure out of dunking on people who you disagree with.

Now, I'm a big girl. I know what I signed up for. I know who I am. There's no crying in baseball. I get paid a lot of money. There are way worse jobs. My brother Jimmy dug sewers in Iraq. I don't want it to seem like I didn't understand my privilege and the level I'm at. But I see brutal comments on my social media every single day: "Fuck you," "I hate you," "You're the worst," "You're a Nazi," "Spoiled, elitist bitch," blah, blah, blah. To say you have to have thick skin to be in this business is putting it extremely mildly. But the thought of my address essentially being handed to the trolls made me very uncomfortable.

When I am uncomfortable, I do my best to find a way to get comfortable again. When it came to that woman essentially printing my address online, I decided to do what I could to remove myself from the situation.

I feel bad for people who haven't been doing this as long as I have and are undone by cruelty online. I also feel sorry for people who don't have the means and capability to change things in their life in a way that they feel safer.

I worry about young people feeling judged on social media. I see it with my nieces, who are fifteen, twenty-one, and twenty-three. They are beautiful, and yet they have distorted perspectives of their bodies and our culture.

The number-one thing I worry about with having a girl is the toxic values we're projecting online onto women and the rampant bullying and harassment. If you're going to be in the public eye in any way, of course you may be subjected to criticism. But what you see online is not just criticism—it's emotional abuse.

So far, I'd rather still be in the kitchen where things are cooking than not, but I have less and less tolerance for it than I ever have before. Since becoming a mother, I have less and less bandwidth. I look at things online, and now I say, "Is this worth it? Does it matter?" Motherhood has put life in perspective in a lot of ways for me, and so has COVID.

That grind of the fight every day, it takes so much out of me. I want to hold my baby and hang out with my husband and talk to my friends. I'm lucky. I have a close unit of friends. I don't have a lot of friends, but those I have, I'm very close to.

I never thought I'd say it, but I want to do other things than just fighting about politics.

Not to mention that women catfighting isn't always necessarily the best look. And while I believe what I do on TV and online is noble debating a lot of the time, sometimes it's cheap and dirty on all of our parts, mine and everybody else's. Since having a daughter, I have nothing to do but hang out with her and think. And there are definitely things about my life engaged in battle on TV and on Twitter that I'm not proud of. Getting pounded on Twitter for having said something about the looting clarified that for me.

The next day after the "It's fine" moment on Twitter, after I found out that *Page Six* was about to post our address in Virginia, I tried to clarify: "I am six months pregnant. A gossip organization is about to run a story of where me and my family are currently. I sent a tweet yesterday based on the news I saw happening in Midtown. We all have been watching over different media platforms. I support the peaceful protests, their movement but am absolutely heartbroken about the destruction in the city I have loved since I moved to when I was eighteen. It is important to have your voice heard and I hope everyone stays safe and healthy."

Well, that added fuel to the fire. People on Twitter crowed, "She's not even in New York!" They suggested that I'd run to Virginia so

I could stockpile guns, which was definitely not the case. We were there because it was easier to shelter in place, and Ben's parents were nearby. I kept my apartment because I was assuming we were going back in a couple of weeks. Then one month passed, two months passed. Ben and I started to begin conversations at home with: "Are we going to go back or what?" Our lease was up in July. I was pushing to keep our apartment. I told Ben, "It's going to be a pain in the ass when they call us back to the show. We should just keep it and keep paying rent."

Ben agreed, and so we'd re-signed the lease a week before the Twitter nightmare. But now I didn't want to stay there. I don't know when I've been more furious. I emailed the management company and I said, "How do you expect me to live here when I have a neighbor who's trying to shame me and telling everyone where I live?"

They let me out of the lease, which was nice of them. A week later, Ben and a friend of mine who owns a moving company went to the apartment and moved us out. I put everything into storage here in the D.C. area. My feeling was: "You don't want people like me in your building? It's okay to loot and riot in your city, and if someone says it's depressing, you pile on them? Great. I'm leaving." I could not have felt less wanted by a city I'd loved for so long.

I know everyone thinks I'm a New York turncoat or something, but I felt like I had no choice.

People like me can afford to leave the city and go someplace else, but all I could think was that people of lower socioeconomic status and the people who own those stores getting busted up, they're the ones who are suffering. And people like me can ride out Twitter rage, but people who are less prepared for it don't have the same recourse. My friend Bari Weiss, who I went to college with, was just harassed out of her job at the *New York Times*.

Twitter mobs are the worst. I'd never partake in them. If AOC lived down the hall from me, I would never tell anyone. I disagree with her on plenty, but I don't hate her. With that *Full Frontal* woman tweeting where I lived, it felt like she *hated* me, like she wanted to unleash the hounds on me and my family.

That period was certainly the most I have ever watched Tucker Carlson in my whole life. That week, everything he was saying, I was agreeing with. He said, "Even if you do what the mob tells you to do, you will not be spared. The people on Twitter are predators. Predators are incited by weakness. They exploit it. The only solution in the face of something like this is to tell the truth unapologetically."

When I think about people struggling to come back from problematic comments, I think about Beto O'Rourke. When he came on *The View*, I asked him about his appearance on the cover of *Vanity Fair*, where he appeared with the pull quote, "I want to be in it. Man, I'm just born to be in it." I also asked him about something he said about his wife: "She is raising, sometimes with my help," their three kids.

That line played poorly, especially with women, who saw a serious double standard. What female politician could have gotten away with saying she helped out with the kids "sometimes"?

When he answered me, it was as if someone had pushed a button on a prerecorded message. In a very practiced voice, he started talking about privilege and about how women of color are paid so much less on the dollar and foundational discrimination and the legacy of slavery and Jim Crow. And in a plodding, contrite voice, he went on and on.

I thought, *This man is never going to be president. That was not a tough question, and this is the worst answer I've ever heard.*

We need to live in a world where someone can say, "I screwed up. I made a dumb error. I'm sorry," and for the conversation to move on. So many people want to fall so hard on the sword that it's debasing. People mess up. It's life. At a certain point, you must be authentic in politics. I didn't think he'd screwed up that badly, but he seemed unable to bounce back from it. It certainly shouldn't have been a kill shot for his campaign. It was amazing to watch a man who'd been hailed as a leading candidate make such a JV mistake.

"I have my work cut out for me," he said, talking in a focus-grouped way about reinforcing narratives of privilege. The camera cut to me, and my brow was furrowed at him. We asked him if his wife hadn't been bothered by what he'd said. He said she told him she knew what he meant and appreciated the sentiment.

Sunny said his wife had gone easy on him.

"You're clearly not married to Meghan or Sunny," I said.

As much as I don't like the overly cautious way Beto handled that slipup, I did understand the fear that led to it. There is an oppressive climate of judgment in public life these days. And I worry that whenever people feel censored, it breeds animosity and discontent. Not to mention that it's downright un-American.

I know people who've lost jobs for being too intense. They might yell at an intern for doing something super wrong, and then they're suddenly banned from the premises. And I understand why such people might become more radical or MAGA types.

Sarah Silverman has said something similar: "If we don't give these people a path to redemption, then they're going to go where they are accepted, which is the . . . dark side." She says without some means of redemption, they're "going to find someplace where they are accepted and it's not going to be with progressives . . . I think there should be some kind of path. Do we want people to be changed? Or do we want them to freeze in a moment we found them on [the] internet from twelve years ago?"

We're pushing people into boxes and into spaces that are sad and dangerous on both sides because we're not listening to one another. I know I'm scared of interacting at all with the woke set. I never know what to say. I always think I'm going to say the wrong thing, and I'm going to make a joke that's going to offend someone and I'm going to get fired. You're walking on eggshells. I know I only want to talk about the weather in a corporate environment because you hear all these stories about everyone reporting one another to HR for the smallest things.

This is the level of absurdity we've reached: Somebody on Bill Maher's show said he made a joke to a woman in an elevator. When she said, "Which floor do you get off on?" he said, "The lingerie floor." She reported him because she thought it was sexually aggressive and violent.

Yes, some people are irredeemable. But an awful lot of people could be returned to society if they were given some way to do it. I'm a forgiver in life in general. I feel like it's healthy for the forgiven and the forgiver. If you're raping someone or assaulting someone or hurting someone, goodbye forever. But if you wrote a stupid tweet twenty-five years ago? I'm not so sure.

A lot of people supported Trump purely because he spoke out so forcefully against political correctness. And when you have kids in college saying, "Oh, you didn't say those words the right way. We're all going to pile on you and make sure you're fired," then anyone opposing them can start to look reasonable.

The conversation around "cancel culture" pushed a lot of uncertain voters toward Trump, as did demands for defunding the police.

I believe we need to have more conversations about racial inequality and police reform. Unarmed Black men keep getting shot for no reason. This is a fact and a national crisis. But over the summer, there was pressure to say that therefore it's okay that these protests were resulting in innocent people getting hurt and in mom-and-pop businesses seeing their storefronts destroyed. We weren't having a conversation anymore about why we need to reform the way police deal with mental illness, for example—it was all this "Calm down, princess" shit and people saying we should be okay with violence because it's justified.

Now you have Democrats like South Carolina congressman James Clyburn coming out to say that the slogans like "Defund the Police" tanked a lot of Democratic candidates. It's the most toxic message ever, and I've been saying it for months.

On *The View*, people would tell me that it didn't mean shut down the police; it meant X, Y, and Z. And I said, "If you're having to explain what your message is in politics, you're losing." Whoopi and Sunny were freaked out by the idea that it was playing poorly with swing voters. They said, "What do you know?"

I said, "I know people are confused. They think you're *trying* to remove the police. And then when someone is trying to invade their home, they'll have no one to call for help. I know you have a Minneapolis City Council president saying on CNN that wanting to call the police when your home gets broken into 'comes from a place of privilege.' That's the kind of thing that could kill the Left going forward."

To this day, I don't get why that Samantha Bee writer tweeted that about me, making fun of me for being sensitive about the neighborhood and outing me as living there, inviting the pile-on. I'd never even met her. I felt like, over the years, I'd given so much to New York. I'm an active member of the community. After that Twitter experience, I felt unwelcome. I felt like I'd basically been kicked out of New York City. It felt like a breakup. I haven't been back since.

I'm still on Twitter, but I try to keep it bland on there as much as possible. And I left Facebook. For a while, I had a private account there, but then all these people from high school were writing strange things and getting in political fights on my wall. I still like Instagram, more or less, but all social media I think of as a weapon. You've got to be careful. You've got to keep the safety on. And now when I go on vacation, I make sure to delete the Twitter app off my phone.

CHAPTER 10

A NEW KIND OF PARTY GIRL

When my father first ran for president, I was twenty-two and still in college. He invited me to a New York City hotel room to sit in on a meeting to plot the announcement of his candidacy. Because there was some concern about his advanced age—he would have been seventy-two when elected—his advisors were trying to convince him that when he announced, he had to say, "I'll only be choosing to serve one term. If elected, it will only be four years and then I'll give the next generation a chance."

To my ears, what that signaled was a lack of confidence and an acknowledgment that his age was a liability, not a strength.

I piped up from the corner of the room: "Excuse me, you should absolutely not do that. It sounds desperate, and I don't think the American public will go for it. It sounds like you're agreeing that what your opponent is saying is true: you're old and not capable of serving eight years. It also sounds like you're predicting the future when you don't know what's going to come."

The room grew tense. His team was furious at me. Mark Salter, my dad's biographer and speechwriter, glared at me. I could see that he was very, very angry.

But my father wanted my opinion. He always wanted my opinion. The other men in the room did not. Their attitude was, *Who's this punk college kid telling this American hero what to do?*

My father ignored the tension in the room and he said, "Huh? You think it sounds desperate?"

"Yeah," I said. "I think it sounds really desperate."

He was quiet for a second, and then he said, "She's right." He took out that part from the speech.

Later, my father's chief of staff, Joe Donoghue, said, "You should be proud of what you did. You stopped him from making a dumb mistake when a team full of so-called experts didn't."

But most of his advisors never forgave me. They tried to ice me out from then on, to keep me out of meetings and conversations, but my father kept pulling me in. I do still think that I was right about the one-term pledge.

I'm often asked questions about my confidence: "How did you get so opinionated so young? How were you so empowered when you were younger?"

When I was a kid and he was running for Senate, he brought me along to everything. As a five-year-old, I tagged along to his interviews at KTAR in Phoenix. I went to hundreds of town halls. I always enjoyed them, because he had a real knack for the format and for finding ways to charm just about everyone. He said that when he lost the election, he slept like a baby: slept two hours and woke up and cried and then slept two hours and woke up and cried. He loved to quote Dick Tuck, who said upon losing his own 1966 California State Senate campaign: "The people have spoken, the bastards."

He liked to tell stories about going into a Phoenix barbershop and saying he was running for president and being told, "Yeah, we were just laughing about that earlier."

If someone was giving him a hard time about not being conservative enough and he got sick of it, he'd say, "It's clear that I'm not your candidate. Next question?"

He wouldn't take unlimited amounts of abuse. But he loved a good debate, and he made me believe in the power of having a lot of disparate voices in the room—including women's voices.

I give his mother, Roberta, credit for teaching him to respect women. Roberta was born in 1912 in Muskogee, Oklahoma. She was a firecracker. She had three children: my dad, his brother, and his sister. She didn't care what anybody thought about her. I love women like that. She was a socialite and kept house for my grandfather, an admiral in the Navy. She wasn't the warmest, most nurturing mother, but she lived by the beat of her own drummer. She was strong and smart and did whatever the hell she wanted. She loved traveling, which she kept up until she was ninety.

When she was eighty-eight, Roberta went to Italy. They told her that she was too old to rent a car—so she bought one instead. My dad used to bring her out on the campaign to prove that he wasn't too old to serve. He'd always said that she gave him endurance genes. I always said that it takes a tough woman to raise a tough man like my dad. In fact, my dad was the least misogynistic man I've ever met in my entire life. He genuinely respected women.

He had a staff full of women of all ages, and he thought the world of my mom. I grew up with a male father figure who never treated me any differently than my brothers. He always respected my opinion. When I first started to experience sexism in the workplace as I got older, I was so surprised. I kept saying, "Oh my God, this still exists? Gross. God, why am I not prepared for this?"

And I saw sexism in full flower when my father chose Sarah Palin as his vice-presidential pick.

No one asks me about Sarah Palin anymore. I find that notable because there was a time in my life when I couldn't go anywhere without people asking about her, and now I never hear her name. It's a short period of time for such a major fall from grace.

My father chose her as his VP running mate in 2008 after they'd spent very little time together. He liked her independent streak. She was supposed to be a mavericky governor. But when she was first chosen in Ohio, their body language was extremely uncomfortable backstage. They had just met and were like strangers.

He was talked into choosing her by the campaign strategist Steve Schmidt. He is now on MSNBC and conspicuously quiet about the fact that he is single-handedly responsible for bringing Sarah Palin into our collective consciousness.

Sarah Palin was a precursor to Trump—and, by the way, one of the only former McCain associates besides me to stay a Republican during the Trump years. She was the first politician to attract this populist, deep-red element of the party. She quickly became more popular than my dad with a different section of the party. There was a group that felt validated and represented by her. And her convention speech was completely brilliant. There was no denying the impact of lines like the famous: "Do you know the only difference between a pit bull and a hockey mom? Lipstick."

In some ways, she got a raw deal. She was plucked from obscurity and thrown into the national spotlight and treated shittily by the mainstream media. Some of it she brought on herself. But looking back on it, a lot of people were violently unkind. There were conspiracy theories about Trig, her infant son with Down's syndrome, not being hers and actually being her grandson. It was sick.

I have more compassion toward her now than I ever had before. Maybe it's because I'm older. Maybe it's because I see more clearly now how women are treated in the media. I think if she weren't so pretty, maybe there would be different conversations about her. One thing I liked about her was that she was the first politician I ever saw with a baby. Trig was a few months old, and she was in her mid-forties.

At the same time, she didn't treat everyone the way she should have. She was so impressed with herself at that time. I think she thought she was invincible, and that she was going to be the next president. Over a period of time, she may have been able to, but she didn't rise to the occasion back then. My dad later wished he had chosen Joe Lieberman because Joe was his best friend, and if he was going to lose, he thought it would have been better to go out with his best friend by his side.

To this day, some of my family's closest friends are Joe and Hadassah Lieberman. The two of them were always around when I was growing up. Joe is an uncle to me. They would join us in Sedona for the Fourth of July. Even though they weren't Republicans, and even though in 2000 Joe was a vice-presidential nominee for the Democratic Party on the ticket with Al Gore, that didn't mean they couldn't be best friends. The important thing to my father was that Joe was a man of decency. He joked that Joe was too decent, in fact, to be in politics.

When the Palins arrived, they brought so much drama with them on the plane from Alaska.

I was on the campaign trail with them, blogging about it as McCain Blogette. One day while looking at gossip sites, I saw on PerezHilton.com that Bristol was pregnant. I went to ask my dad's press secretary if it was true. She was a chain-smoker, and I found her outside his bus smoking. She took a drag and said, "Yup."

"Well, what the hell is everybody going to do?" I asked.

From what I could tell, a lot of people were caught off guard by that piece of information. And it felt like the Palins were daring us to say anything about it. I felt like they didn't show my father all that much respect.

Bristol would go on to talk a lot of shit about me and my mom in her 2011 memoir, *Not Afraid of Life*. I didn't read it, but a friend of mine sent me some excerpts. She said I was "constantly checking us out, comparing my family to hers and complaining. Oh, the complaining." She complained that my mother was presumptuous to offer herself and my father as godparents for her baby.

As proof, she recounts a moment in the convention hotel's hair-and-makeup room in which, on my way to a campaign photo shoot, with bare face and wet hair, I got bumped for the entire

Palin brigade, including Levi and seven-year-old Piper. For the record, those little kids were angels. Willow and Piper and the little ones were adorable, with perfect manners. Levi and Bristol, on the other hand, were incredibly rude to me and to everyone on the McCain team.

As was widely reported, the RNC spent $150,000 on head-to-toe makeovers for the whole Palin family. And on this particular day, the hairstylist told me that she didn't fit me in because the Palins, frankly, would be getting "more airtime."

It burned, but it was true. In her book, Bristol took me to task for cursing and stomping out at that point to go do my own hair and makeup, and said I'd been marinating in politics for too long. She said that she hoped *she* would "avoid the fate of being obsessed with the political spotlight."

A few years later, I saw her at the White House Correspondents' Dinner. Bristol ran away from me before I could say hello. That wasn't necessary. I don't bear her any ill will. To me, it's a sad political story. Given how the campaign went and what happened afterward, I often wonder: Did my dad make Sarah Palin's career or ruin her life? Would it have been better for her and everyone in 2008 if they'd stayed in Alaska?

In the past decade, they've done multiple reality shows, and their personal lives have been splashed all over the tabloids. Sarah appeared on *The Masked Singer*, and her thirty-plus-year marriage to Todd ended during the pandemic. Their eldest son, Track, has been in trouble with the law repeatedly.

Bristol has done *Dancing with the Stars* twice and her own show, *Bristol Palin: Life's a Tripp*. She's pitched herself repeatedly to replace me on *The View*. The demise of her relationships with her children's fathers has played out publicly. Tripp's father, Levi Johnston, wrote his own book trash-talking the McCains and the Palins. It's called *Deer in the Headlights*, which is appropriate because from my experience with him on the trail, he was very cocky because he'd been hot shit in his tiny town but out in the world was dumber than plywood. He posed nude in *Playgirl*, and his sister Mercede posed in *Playboy*. She kept a blog that was basically a Bristol Palin hate site. The military-hero father of Bristol's daughters she accused online of not deserving his Medal of Honor.

And yet, for all the speed bumps and tensions, I have nothing but beautiful memories of the experience being on the road with the campaign. I had a couple of my friends along for the ride with me, and we had a great time hanging out in one motel after another, joking around with staffers, and learning about the inner workings of the political process. Now I know how precious that time was for our country, too. My father and Obama respected each other. The debates were civil, and so, for the most part, was the electorate.

I was so proud when my father spoke up for Obama even against his own supporters if they were trying to suggest that Obama was a dangerous man.

"I have to tell you . . . [Obama] is a decent person and a person that you do not have to be scared [of] as president of the United States . . . He's a decent family man, [and] citizen that I just happen to have disagreements with on fundamental issues. And that's what this campaign is all about."

My dad was so amazingly patient and kind to let me join him and be around him. He made it seem as though I boosted his morale. I always felt like I was there to keep him entertained and happy and having fun. That was my job. My secondary job was the blog, which in theory was helping him reach out to younger voters, up to a point. It was certainly before its time. It's cheesy and very embarrassing now. But I was glad I had a purpose.

Back in those days, I reached a real fork in the road. Down one path was a career, and down the other path was nonstop partying. The party girl was an amoeba version of who I am now, and I made a lot of dumb mistakes. Every misstep I made—and plenty I didn't!—seemed to wind up in gossip columns.

The media was hard on me for a long time. Everyone wanted to cast me as a dumb, spoiled trust-fund kid with no business doing anything or saying anything. Some of that vitriol I earned, but most of it I didn't. Because of my experience at that time, I always give young people grace now, whether it's an intern on the show who makes a mistake or Sasha Obama being slammed for dancing on TikTok.

I had so much fun in my early twenties. I was definitely a party girl. I never did drugs; they always scared me. Addiction runs in my family. Also, from a vanity perspective, I didn't want to start looking the way people look when they do drugs. But it's fair to say I was not taking life seriously.

For my father, the straw that broke the camel's back was a picture of me drinking with Tila Tequila in L.A. when I was twenty-three.

People outside of my generation might not know who she is, but she was a Myspace star and had her own bisexual dating show on MTV. I don't even remember how we became friends, but we used to hang out sometimes. And one night we went out to a boozy dinner, and somebody took pictures of us. In an interview, she then implied we were having an affair. Even though my family wouldn't have minded it if I was gay, they did not like these debauched images of me partying all over the internet.

My dad called me and said, "What are you doing? Is this what you want? You have a platform. You've been given all these gifts, and you're privileged. You don't want people to think you're a spoiled brat."

Being a spoiled brat was basically the worst thing you could be to him. He hated it. I think it's because he grew up so tough and did so many hard things. He hated people using economic privilege in a way that was ostentatious.

His disappointment in me was palpable. This was right around the same time that Bristol Palin was doing reality television, and I was offered every single reality show that exists, from *Dancing with the Stars* to dumb dating stuff.

Around 2012, Trump called me personally to ask me to come on *The Apprentice*. He told me how amazing the show was and how I had to do it. He kept saying if I did the show, I "would be a winner." My only distinct memory of the call is that he used the word *winner* over and over again.

I never took any of the show offers, fortunately, because I'm more private than I think the average person on TV is. Still, to this day, whenever I see a celebrity embarrassing themselves on a reality show, I think, *There but for the grace of God go I.* To me, that year was a real *Sliding Doors* moment. Were it not for my father's intervention, I could have gone down a very different path.

That summer, I went home for a visit to Sedona, and my father sat me down. He said, "You're making a jackass of yourself. I'm getting phone calls, and I don't like it." He was very matter-of-fact. He said, "You can make the decision of what you want to do with your life, because you're grown. Is this what you want your life to be like? Just a dumbass who parties? You know that everybody's embarrassed for you. They're not saying it, because they're being polite, but everyone's embarrassed. Fly straight."

That's what he always said when he was disappointed: "Fly straight."

"Oh my God," I said, genuinely shocked by this news. "I'm sorry! I'm an asshole!"

I did clean up my act. It's not like I entered a nunnery. But I stopped being stupid publicly as much as possible. I started trying to be more serious.

I think he was right that I had to watch what I did and who saw it. It's very dangerous to start going down a path where, sadly, perception is reality. If you're seen as someone who's only partying and saying dumb things and going out all the time, I think it can become the truth because no one will ever give you the chance to become more.

Fortunately, once I started flying straighter, I found incredible mentors who kept me on track. One was Jon Meacham, who I worked for at *Newsweek* when I was in college. He was the best boss I ever had. He was deeply respectful, even of the interns and the young writers. The mood was collaborative. I haven't met that many people in the workforce, in general, who seek out and listen to young voices. People blow off young people as a rule. But Jon let all the interns write for the magazine. And he would have lunches where we would all ask him questions and he would ask us questions. He's from Tennessee, and I remember that felt so different at the time because most people were from New York or Boston. It was the most fun job I ever had. I still ask him for advice from time to time.

My other mentor is Harris Faulkner at Fox News. She's my TV mentor. She hosts two shows on Fox, and she's the only full-time Black female weekday anchor on Fox News. When I first got to Fox, I was intimidated. I felt like I was way younger than I am now. I wasn't that young. I was thirty. But it feels like twenty lifetimes ago. I started cohosting *Outnumbered*, a show on Fox featuring four women and then one guy. Harris taught me how to read the prompter better, and she would give constructive criticism about everything from my delivery to my hair and makeup. She was very collaborative and encouraging, and we had a lot in common because her dad was in the military and her husband is from Arizona.

She's my go-to example of how to support other women, and for how to be ladylike and regal while also being tough as nails. She did not feel threatened at all by up-and-coming young people. I knew she knew her own power and refused to see other women as competition: "I host all these shows. I'm Harris Faulkner. I can do whatever I want. Come in, join or not." To this day, she's still someone that I go to for career advice every time there's a crisis.

When people bring up my old tweets, I'll admit, "Yeah, it was dumb." But talking about taking a fireball shot is not the same thing as some of the other stuff people have done. So, let's put things in perspective. The reason I'm so content with my place in my life now is because I got all that partying out of my system. I don't feel like I'm missing out because I've done so many fun things.

I made a lot of good friendships over the years with media people who I rely on now in a much more serious way. I'll call them for background on a guest we're having, or I'll ask them to explain a complicated political situation to me.

One friend from my partying days was on the ground in 2020 reporting on Black Lives Matter and COVID, and I was grateful to him for his insights and firsthand accounts of what was happening. Those relationships I made early on that were based purely on having fun have grown into associations that are professionally useful now.

My father, Jon Meacham, and Harris Faulkner all helped me become a grown-up. But for years, I'd still get treated by some older men as a joke.

The famous book about the 2008 presidential election, *Game Change*, was written by Mark Halperin and John Heilemann. They were the cool kids of political media at the time, and everyone who leaked on my dad's campaign went to them.

Obviously, I hated them. *Game Change* is mean and inaccurate. To take one example, there's something in the book about how my dad walked around in his underwear around people, which he never did. To say he was a modest man is putting it mildly. Part of the reason he was reluctant to even wear a bathing suit is because he had scars all over his body, wounds of war. I just went online to see if I could find a picture of him without a shirt on, and I couldn't.

A lot of ex-staffers like Nicolle Wallace and Steve Schmidt felt that they needed to reinvent themselves after my dad lost, and so they fed *Game Change* with stories casting themselves as innocent bystanders in a loser's campaign brought down by crazytown Sarah

Palin. I didn't end up reading the entire book. I read two-thirds of it and then said, "Nope," and put it down. I watched part of the movie but couldn't finish that either.

During the 2012 RNC, I was in my twenties and working for MSNBC. One day when I was about to go on *Hardball* with Chris Matthews, I was backstage, and *Game Change* author Mark Halperin was there. I didn't like him, but didn't want to be rude to him, so I greeted him in a friendly way. As best I can recall it, this was the conversation that followed.

"Hi, Mark Halperin," I said.

He didn't say anything. I thought he didn't hear me.

"Hi! How are you, Mark Halperin?"

He didn't say anything.

"Do we have an issue?" I said.

He said, in a low, menacing voice, "Are you going to be a brat?"

"What?" I said.

"I'm not going to speak to you if you're going to be a brat. Are you going to act like that? I know the things you've been saying."

He went *off* on me, his every word dripping in misogyny and condescension.

I was taken aback. He might have heard I didn't love the trashy book he'd done about my father, but that hardly seemed like a reason to talk to me like I was a stupid child.

"What?" was the only word I could fit in as he read me to filth.

I was humiliated and shaken. That's a hard thing to do to me.

A producer who was there came over and intervened.

This was *ten* years ago, but I still remember the panic I felt: "What did I do? What's going on?"

Normally, I don't feel constrained by my gender. But that was one time in which I was certain he would never have talked to a man like that.

After the media spot, at dinner with a friend, I said, "I can't believe he gets away with talking like that."

But times change, and his manner of speaking to young women has gone out of fashion. Cut to Mark Halperin getting fired from NBC and MSNBC for, among other things, pressing his erect penis against at least one woman while he worked at ABC News. His behavior has been well documented, and there are ample testimonials from women about how uncomfortable he's made them. When these stories came out, I thought, *Guess I got off easy.*

As far as I can tell, he doesn't have a career anymore. He had to split with his collaborator, John Heilemann, who still works on a Showtime show called *The Circus* that my friend produces.

That moment with Mark Halperin is one of those times that will always stick out in my memory as a fork in the road. He fought against my being in that room, and I had to fight to stay in it. Again, whether or not he thought I should be in that room with him, MSNBC thought I should. It wasn't his call. As much as it rattled me, I was able to pull myself together and go out on the set and do my job.

There will always be people who see me as an entitled, one-percenter brat, no matter what I do. Every room I go in, that's the preconception. It's up to me to work hard enough to convince people that I deserve to be there. I know that and I accept it. But I took exception to this person who had made money peddling what I considered fictions about my family calling me that in a greenroom.

One good thing to say about *Game Change* is that it's a relic of an earlier era.

And it's a valuable reminder that the rise of social media has had at least one positive effect: it's meant that guys like Mark Halperin and John Heilemann aren't the only gatekeepers anymore. That's a good thing. Political discourse shouldn't be about an elitist club relegated to certain people voicing a particular perspective.

You can be a young renegade reporter and create your own platform. If people do good work and then put it out there themselves, it's respected, and it's seen. Social media is an equalizing force.

If I saw a man screaming at a young political woman who was about to go on-air, I would lose my mind, and I would stop it. I'd probably start recording it on my phone and put it on Twitter. So, I'm glad we're living in a time in which there are repercussions for bad behavior. But it's sad that there were men who felt like it was always okay to talk to women like that and got away with it for so many years.

Politics is hindered by not having enough journalists of different backgrounds. Back in the days of *Game Change*, the conversation was so one-note. A lot of political TV still is. But, little by little, there's a shift occurring, and there are other voices in the room.

CHAPTER 11

THE PRESIDENT IS CALLING

My father called me on election night when Trump had won.

"Are you in your apartment?" he said.

"Yes," I replied.

"Good. Go to the window. Quick! Go look outside."

"Why?"

"Just stand up and go look outside your window."

"Okay, I'm looking outside the window," I said.

"Do you see all those fucking pigs flying around?"

I laughed so hard. But I knew that his joke came from a place of pain. He'd worked so hard for bipartisanship, and it felt like that dream would now be dead for at least four years. The Trump years were scary for a lot of reasons, and so uncertain. I never knew if he was going to, say, nuke Sweden because of a tweet about Trump Steaks.

After my father died, Trump's rhetoric grew even more vicious. Then COVID arrived. I wasn't surprised when I saw that the country was experiencing a Zoloft shortage. Reading the news, I would think, *Dad's not missing much. Things went to hell.* This is terrible to say, but I'm almost relieved he didn't live to see this era in American history. I also had this thought that he would have been impossible to keep quarantined. He hated being in one place for any length of time.

President Trump called me three years ago, when my father was sick. Trump had made another cruel comment about him—at this point, I can't even remember which one because he did it almost compulsively—and I'd tweeted: "What more must my family be put through?"

I got a phone call: "This is the White House. President Trump would like to speak with you."

Rather than responding right away, I called my dad first.

"Trump's trying to call me," I said. "I don't want to talk to him."

"You have to talk to him," my dad said. "He's the president of the United States. I don't care who he is; you can't blow off the president of the United States."

So, I took the call. Trump didn't apologize, but he said the reporting was wrong. I just stayed quiet and listened to him talk. Then Melania got on the other line and said, "We love you! We love your dad!"

"No, you don't," I said.

It was the weirdest experience, because Trump had said so many things on the record trashing my dad, and now he was telling me that I shouldn't be mad about it. He wouldn't change his tactics, either. He would go on to talk about my father over and over again, always in derogatory ways.

While he was campaigning for president in 2015, Trump said of my father, "He's not a war hero. He was a war hero because he was captured. I like people who weren't captured." For years, he made a sport of beating the crap out of my family, and he didn't let up once he got into the Oval Office. Trump had supporters boo my father at a rally. He fought the lowering of the flag in my dad's honor when he died. It was extremely emotionally taxing.

On the day I'm writing this, I'm looking at a tweet from Trump: "Check out last in his class John McCain, one of the most overrated people in D.C."

I thought, *Go to sleep, asshole. It's twelve thirty at night.*

Then I replied to the tweet: "Two years after he died, you still obsess over my dad. It kills you that no one will ever love you or remember you like they loved and remember him. He served his country with honor. You have disgraced the office of the presidency."

Then I added, because I couldn't help myself, "You couldn't even pull it out in Arizona . . ."

My grievance was great because of how much harder Trump made everything. Whenever I began to have time and space to mourn my father, Trump would pop up to say something terrible about him. Every commentator would have a response to the comments, and I'd have to hear them played out over and over again. This cycle was so gross and so macabre it actually stunted my ability to mourn. It was like having a scab ripped off again and again so that a wound couldn't heal. It wreaked emotional havoc on my family. And no matter how many times he did it, it never stopped being painful.

It was pretty delicious irony when Trump lost Arizona in 2020. I'm not saying it's *only* because he trash-talked my father, who is extremely popular in his home state. Another factor was that Arizona got hit hard with COVID, especially the Native American population on reservations. But it felt like karma. Watching the returns come in as I held Liberty in my arms, I imagined how mad Trump would have been to have lost a red state, and I laughed.

"It sucks to suck!" I said to Trump's stern face on the electoral map.

I confess that I also enjoyed the meme that showed a picture of my father with the line underneath: "I like people who don't lose Arizona."

There was a related political cartoon of my father and civil rights hero John Lewis of Georgia, who Trump also attacked repeatedly. They were clad in suits and angel wings, halos over their heads, looking down on Earth from a cloud, fist-bumping. Many people wrote to me to say: "Your dad's in heaven, and he made Arizona go for Biden!"

I wrote back: "I appreciate the sentiment, but I sincerely hope that's not what my dad's doing in the afterlife. I hope that he's having more fun than that."

I loved my father more than I ever loved anyone other than my husband or my child. We were very alike and had a special bond. He was not perfect. He never presented himself as that, but he's turned into this cult saint figure, especially in contrast with Trump.

I hope that a passion for fair, goals-oriented political conversation is something that the Trump years did not kill. I hope other people growing up now can love political discourse the same way I do. Because if I grew up in this climate, I fear I'd see it as angry and dark and visceral and ugly in a way that it never was when I was young.

When Trump was refusing to concede, I was glad to see my father's concession speech circulating as a contrasting example of a classy way to bow out. In his speech, he talked about how important it was that President Obama was elected and what a great man he was and how important it was, especially for people of color, to have that barrier broken.

He said:

> In a contest as long and difficult as this campaign has been, his success alone commands my respect for his ability and perseverance. But that he managed to do so by inspiring the hopes of so many millions of Americans, who had once wrongly believed that they had little at stake or little influence in the election of an American president, is something I deeply admire and commend him for achieving. This is an historic election, and I recognize the special significance it has for African Americans and for the special pride that must be theirs tonight.

How gracious, and how unlike the tone of the last four years.

I understood why fans of my father put pressure on me in 2016 and 2020 to honor him by coming out more viscerally and actively against Trump. I was not a fan of Trump, but I also believe that anytime you let someone or something consume your entire psyche, it's not healthy.

My strategy was to call Trump out for cruelty and to vote against him, but to try not to lose my mind or panic. I believed the conservative party would return to its fundamentals eventually. I remember hearing one left-wing pundit talking about how, on her honeymoon, all she could talk about was Trump. I said, "Do what you're supposed to be doing on your honeymoon! Why are you talking about Trump?"

So many people have built their careers on hating Trump. What identity crisis is going to happen in the media now? I always think the biggest con Trump ever pulled was turning people into him. By making them angry enough, he transformed formerly stable people into monsters who think nothing of dehumanizing others. And then they're so obsessed with him, they can't think or talk about anything else.

Plenty of people on the Left who I genuinely like said that anyone who voted for Trump is racist and selfish. But there are a lot of Trump voters out there who can't afford to put their kids into a good school or even to put food on the table every night. They lost all faith in the people who were in power before him. The idea that a poor person is supposed to focus on trans rights or climate change when they're in dire straits? It's insulting.

I wasn't as surprised by Trump's win as everyone else was because I was listening to people who I didn't agree with. And I believed what I saw rather than dismissing it as impossible. At the 2016 Republican National Convention in Ohio, I saw Trump signs everywhere, and I felt actual kinetic energy in the convention halls that I hadn't felt before. One of the nights I was there, I was over-come with fear that he could win. It seemed insane that America would pick a reality-show star, but I saw that Trump worked the crowd like a rock star, or a televangelist. His disciples were *his*. I hadn't seen enthusiasm like that for Hillary. I went back to my hotel room and said to Ben, "He might just pull this off. What the *hell* are we going to do?"

The 2016 election was the culmination of middle-American anger toward the media and toward people who didn't take them seriously. An awful lot of people in 2016 felt hopeless. They felt like they had no job and no future. Then there comes Trump, with all his trappings of wealth, saying, "I understand you."

I always think the best line Trump ever used is, "In reality they're not after me. They're after you. I'm just in the way." That's a line that works on *me*. I get it. What he's saying is that even if you hate him, he's a buffer between you and the people who are *really* bad—the craziest parts of the Left, the ones who call you deplorable and who don't even bother to come to your part of the country. This is what the Never-Trumpers of today don't understand.

When I was a kid, the Democratic coalition included the whole sweep of American life, from New York City progressives to prairie populists in the heartland, to southern conservatives in the Deep South. The Democratic Party of that era could speak for the farmer, the worker, and the intellectual aristocracy. Republicans, too, had a broad coalition. If you were a Boston financier, a Midwestern farmer, or a shopkeeper in the West, you could be a Republican.

Now all that is nearly gone. We instead have two parties that represent, for the most part, radically different views of what the

United States is *for*. Two major parties with different views of policy are normal, and survivable, and very ordinary in the life of the republic. Two parties representing *irreconcilable ways of life* constitute an existential threat. The stakes are perceived to be immeasurably higher when your rival is someone not merely with whom you disagree, but someone with whom you have *nothing in common*. Every election is perceived as if it may be the last.

So why has this happened? Well, if you talk to partisans, whether Republican or Democrat, they tend to offer easy answers. Democratic partisans tend to believe the Republicans became a racist party of white people. Republican partisans tend to believe that the Democrats became an anti-American party of elites.

The truth is that as parties have risen, the great institutions of our civic life have fallen. When those institutions fall, so does our common national life and understanding. A civic rite like voting used to transcend our differences; in this new era of polarization, it serves as a mechanism for exacerbating divisions. Today we live in an America where *party identification* predicts civic behavior. It didn't used to be this way. It used to be that on election day, political scientists, consultants, and commentators would look at myriad factors—income, education, even the weather—and try to discern what Americans would do at the ballot box. The assumption was that a great civic consensus existed somewhere in the middle of the people, and we had to discern it.

There was a time when Americans were much more involved with one another across party lines. People in the middle class joined community groups, whether it was the Rotary, the Elks, bingo at the VFW, fish fries at the American Legion, or services at their local church or synagogue. They talked to people who they didn't agree with about everything. People who voted differently went to church together, showed up at the same PTA meetings, and helped each other out. If you broke your leg and couldn't mow your lawn, a neighbor would help you out even if they weren't for your candidate. They weren't siloed off in their own worlds, watching their own media.

There are some things that transcend politics and *ought* to. My friendship with President Biden isn't rooted in our political beliefs but in our common experiences of sorrow. We both know the pain of personal loss. I know him to be both decent and compassionate. That said, I look forward to a time when baby boomers are not in charge.

It feels like the world's a mess, they're not doing a great job with it, and they're never going to leave power. It's going to be up to us, the next generation, to pay for all the spending we're doing now, and so it also should be up to us to take power and restore the country.

My father was friends with Biden and with Hillary Clinton, too. He and Hillary disagreed about everything from foreign policy to the economy, but he never said a bad word about her. When I asked him about his affection for her, given that they'd clashed over everything from the economy to the Iraq War, he simply said, "Meghan, she's a great time."

According to my dad, when the cameras were off, she was funny and interesting and loved nothing more than a night spent drinking and laughing with friends from both sides of the aisle. One of the casualties of the Trump years is that many of us have lost that ability to pal around with our ideological opposite. One day at *The*

View, a producer mentioned that we should try to find a Trump supporter for something. I was the only person in the room who knew *even one*. I knew a ton and rattled off contact information for them until the producer cried uncle.

This bipartisanship may be even less common among Democrats. I know plenty of conservatives who read the *New York Times* but almost no liberals who expose themselves to conservative media like *National Review, Daily Wire*, or *The Federalist*.

It's hard to get out of our own echo chambers, especially because of Twitter. I had a very normal upbringing in Phoenix, all things considered. I went to an all-girls Catholic school, where I did what I was told and played by the rules, for the most part. And then I moved to New York City. I get that New York City has become an avatar for liberalism, but to me, it's an example of what's best about America. It's a melting pot where you can be anything you want. I went to Columbia and had the best time. I interned at *Saturday Night Live* and at *Newsweek*. I credit my pretty normal and happy high school and college experience with the fact that *it all happened pre–social media*.

My dad spoke at one of the Columbia graduations when I was an underclassman. He was booed and protested, and I was so confused at the time as to why. And it was the beginning of my understanding of cancel culture. Matthew Fox from *Lost* was my graduation speaker. And even he was protested. On the Columbia blog, an editor wrote, "We want a Class Day speaker that has accomplished more than being hot and lucking into a role on a show . . . In light of his comparative lack of credibility, Fox's invitation to speak should be rescinded."

My heart goes out to young people today. I can't imagine being a young person, having everything documented and every mistake you make online forever. I believe that Twitter has led to cancel culture, so that everyone is guilty until proven innocent and no one is given the benefit of the doubt. That's not to say that I'm able to stay away from it for long. I'm addicted to Twitter even though I know it's killing me.

Sometimes I feel like Twitter is the cafeteria for people in media and people who work in media and politics and entertainment. Sometimes I see it spread incredible, wonderful things. Sometimes it makes me laugh. And very often, it feels like it makes people abusive to one another. It's a vessel for abuse. I watched the anti–social media documentary *The Social Dilemma*, and it scared the shit out of me, but I had to admit that I'm too far gone. I already did everything wrong.

I've messed up on Twitter twenty million times. I used to drunk-tweet when I was in my early twenties. Once I accidentally tweeted a picture that was meant for a boyfriend—my boobs in a low-cut top. That went viral when I was twenty-four. Most people have forgotten about that, finally, a decade later.

What I've learned is that you have to treat Twitter like a weapon, with the same care you'd bring to a knife or gun—that's how dangerous I think Twitter is. It's a cesspool, and people are disgusting. People have ruined their lives and careers on Twitter.

And yet, for as dangerous and vicious as Twitter is, it's also an important tool. You don't need press people or PR people when you have Twitter. You can say what you want. I like that it's eliminated the need to have people speaking for you, which, especially at *The View*, I don't need.

We can't afford to ignore it. Big Tech is going to be the next real battleground for the culture war. You're already seeing it with Twitter trying to de-platform conservative voices. There doesn't seem to be a lot of continuity about who's censored and who is not.

And I believe that social media is going to stoke antagonism between people even under a Biden presidency. His second year in power, I predict, is going to be a feeding frenzy. The media and the hard Left are going to go for him—start your clock—an hour after Inauguration Day, the second debate starts on the Green New Deal. And that's the Democrats. We're naïve if we think all the Republicans are going to rally around Biden just because he called for healing.

I go on the show every day knowing that many people in the country have literally no one speaking to or for them. Even if I do a poor job of it, at least I'm trying to see them and hear them. As a result, some moderates see me as Trump-sympathetic. I always say, "I'm not Trump-sympathetic. I'm Trump-supporter sympathetic." I don't think you can dismiss seventy-four million people as delusional.

I always feel like I don't perfectly represent red America because, in a lot of ways, I'm in the dreaded 1 percent. I've lived off and on in New York City and the Washington, D.C., Beltway, and I work in media. There are a lot of things about my background that don't fit in at all with the average member of the Right. I try to be extremely cognizant of this group of people and be as sensitive and delicate as possible because it's a huge responsibility to present a position that departs from the one you hear most often on network television. Being the lone conservative woman on a mainstream show is a lot of pressure. I don't perfectly represent red America, but I don't fit in media circles either.

If we showcased truly diverse voices on the news, I believe that people wouldn't have been as surprised by Trump's election in 2016 or by his narrow loss in 2020. More than seventy million people voted for him in the last election. Why am I the only person on a major network who even tries to understand where they're coming from and who speaks for them when we're interviewing public figures?

People want to believe that with Biden as president, the country will become less polarized, but to me, it looks like it might get even worse.

I have a friend named John who's always fighting the good fight for moderates. He wrote a book about how the real pathway is one of independence and centrism. I always say that he's fighting an incredibly noble fight . . . that is not working at all. It's a nice idea and a beautiful sentiment, but there's no coalition for polite centrism.

Without hatred of Trump to unite them, the Left is fractured. Biden's calling for healing, but even among the far Left, I don't see a willingness to meet in the middle. The Squad attacked no less than President Obama over the "Defund the Police" slogan. President Obama said, correctly, that the battle cry didn't work and turned off voters. The Squad told him that he was essentially being insensitive to police brutality victims.

Congresswoman Ilhan Omar tweeted: "We lose people in the hands of the police. It's not a slogan but a policy demand. And centering the demand for equitable investments and budgets for communities across the country gets us progress and safety."

Congresswoman Ayanna Pressley tweeted: "The murders of generations of unarmed Black folks by police have been horrific. Lives are at stake daily so I'm out of patience with critiques of the language of activists. Whatever a grieving family says is their truth. And I'll never stop fighting for their justice & healing."

Normally, congresspeople are very deferential to whoever came before them, the people who helped build the house they're living in. But the members of the Squad don't seem to be at all interested in doing that. Before the ballot recounts were even finished, Speaker Nancy Pelosi and Congresswoman Alexandria Ocasio-Cortez began bickering in public. AOC is on the cover of *Vanity Fair* as I write this. Her policies are very extreme. They alienate a lot of people in this country. And when it comes to working in tandem with her elders like Pelosi, she's very defiant—it's her way or no way.

My beliefs aren't in line with the Left at all, but neither are they compatible with the populist wave that, thanks to Trump, overtook the Republican Party. Over the past few years, I've been feeling like an endangered animal or a relic from the past. I'm holding on to my Republican affiliation, but I think we have a lot of work to do to rebuild the party.

I was a registered independent for a long time. I hated Bush when I was in college. I thought he and Karl Rove were planting the seeds of what would ultimately lead to the Tea Party and then to Trumpism—demonizing the other side in a way that was unprecedented. There's a clear pathway of how we got to Trump: Bush, the Tea Party, then the cultural division that was fostered and exploited under the Obama administration. I think what shouldn't be next is abandoning ship and becoming Democrats. It frustrates me to no end that people think hating Trump means you become a Democrat. That exodus makes me feel very alone, like I'm the only one who believes in the tenets of the Republican Party, and who wants to keep it alive.

As much as I like Joe Biden personally, and I do think he's a kind person, he's not the great inspirational figure of my life. When I see who he's putting in his cabinet, it doesn't feel like there are a lot of new ideas. It feels like a placeholder, a calm way to transition away from Trump.

I'm hoping for new blood in the coming years. Right now, our culture and politics bypass this younger generation of people. It's not that there's something wrong with older people, but I think it's time for some younger energy. Even though I don't like AOC's ideas, she's representing a bunch of people who aren't being represented, and she's not seventy-eight.

Trump is finally gone. The question now that he's gone is: What's next?

CHAPTER 12

MY PARTY'S FUTURE

★ ★ ★

One of my favorite pictures shows my first real foray into politics, in 1986 at the age of two. With my hair in pigtails, I am sitting in between the senator from Arizona, Barry Goldwater, and the man who he was endorsing to replace him, my dad. My dad looks like he's laughing at the skewed ribbon in my hair, while Goldwater looks through his trademark thick black glasses and smiles.

It's the picture of an old Arizona maverick passing the torch to a new one.

My father said that Goldwater, who ran unsuccessfully for president in 1964, "transformed the Republican Party from an Eastern elitist organization to the breeding ground for the election of Ronald Reagan."

The conservative columnist George Will—no fan of my dad's—wrote of Reagan's 1980 victory that Goldwater actually won in '64—it just took sixteen years to count the votes.

It's a hard thing for most of us to remember, but there was a time when the Republican Party wasn't the vehicle for populism it is today. Goldwater was a big part of changing that. But he was also, like my father, someone who bucked convention and stubbornly refused to bend to pressures on his principles.

Goldwater was an arch-conservative and anti-communist, remembered for saying "extremism in the defense of liberty is no vice," but he was also a political rule-breaker with friends across the aisle. He was so personally close to John F. Kennedy that, prior to his assassination, the two had agreed to embark on a series of Lincoln–Douglas-style debates across the country. He was a strong defender of gun rights (with the exception of semiautomatic weapons), but when it came to gays in the military, he famously said, "You don't need to be 'straight' to fight and die for your country. You just need to shoot straight."

Today, the upper-crust, snooty northeastern Grand Old Party is long gone. While the party lost upper-class voters to the Democrats in recent years, the GOP has transformed into the most working-class coalition it's been since Ronald Reagan in 1984. The question now is: Where do we go from here? What will the world look like when Liberty is my age? What *should* it look like? And how do we get there?

The overwhelming feeling I've had since the pandemic and insurrection is that the baby boomers have completely failed us in every conceivable way. So many people in that generation acted only in their own self-interest, and we're paying the price now in our addiction to rage and polarization. I hope we can be better, especially when it comes to race.

In the summer of 2020, pregnant and quarantining, I sat at home watching America light itself on fire. And I felt called to reckon with how much unconscious bias I'd had. Because I'd only had good experiences with the police, I'd assumed police brutality wasn't a massive issue. Faced with the protests of 2020 and the powerful testimonies that emerged from it—in a 2020 op-ed, Condoleezza Rice called on each of us to take personal responsibility for fighting prejudice—I became aware of my own ignorance.

When you have Senator Tim Scott saying he's been pulled over seven times in one year for driving while Black, and my cohost Sunny talking about being followed when shopping in department stores, it's clear that there *is* something very different, and very hard, about being Black in America. No one can argue otherwise, though Donald Trump certainly tried.

I think a lot about why, for so long, Trump succeeded politically where so many other Republicans failed. Besides my father, the Republicans who lost presidential elections in my lifetime pre-2016—George H. W. Bush, Bob Dole, Mitt Romney—are all men I respect and, of course, would trust around my daughter. I can't say that of Donald Trump. So, why did the country reject them and support him?

The big part of winning is finding a message that works. Say what you will of Trump, but his message in 2016 was perfectly tuned to the frustrations of so many American voters fed up with a system that they felt they couldn't trust and that they believed had been corrupted and twisted against them. In Trump, they saw a traitor to his class—a rich man who was hated by the same rich, urban people who looked down on them and the values they shared with him.

Faced with a decision between one of the most unpopular candidates ever nominated and a wild card, America chose the wild card. And, boy, did they get one.

We all know the downside of this—four years of a White House and an administration flying by the seat of its pants wasn't good for the country's blood pressure. The Trump administration did a ton of crazy things that I hated. But once in a while, they also did crazy things that were right, maybe because they didn't know they were crazy to do it.

Foreign policy is deeply important to me, and I particularly care about one of America's closest allies in the Middle East, Israel. It was an ally treated terribly under the Obama administration, which undermined its prime minister, Benjamin Netanyahu, at every turn. The Trump administration followed through on several long-held Republican agenda items to support Israel, including moving our embassy from Tel Aviv to Jerusalem.

This is good for America and good for Israel, and it infuriated Obama's former foreign policy team. One Jewish longtime supporter of my father and Republican causes told my husband: "I gave all that money to George W. Bush, and he didn't move the embassy." It's proof that sometimes being a little crazy is what you have to be to get things done over the objections of the experts.

My father was all about that. But he was also a man who respected the lessons of history. He was a Goldwater Republican, through and through. He would work across the aisle, but he wouldn't sacrifice his principles to do so. His career is marked by fiscal conservatism, social traditionalism, and a strong national defense—which political professors call the "three-legged stool" of conservatism in America.

Whenever someone tells you my dad was a liberal, remind them he had top ratings from pro-lifers and the NRA. He may have been the media's favorite conservative. But he was a conservative. And so am I.

When people ask me where we go from here, what the Republican Party becomes post-Trump, I think there's no going back. The bell can't be unrung. "Normal" conservatism in the H. W. Bush, Bob Dole, and Mitt Romney style didn't work. And sadly, my dad's "Maverick" style of conservatism didn't work either at a national level. Trumpism worked, so I expect we'll get more of it—just maybe without the out-of-control tweets.

When my father was running for president, the media shifted in their treatment of him. They had loved him in 2000 as a challenger to the foregone candidate, George W. Bush. But in 2008, especially after he chose Sarah Palin as his vice-presidential pick, they went through a period of absolutely hating him.

Today everyone, even on the Left, wants to talk about my father's greatness. And yet, one thing I can't forget is how my father was demonized at the time just because he was a Republican. They went from celebrating his maverick temperament to suggesting he couldn't be trusted with the nuclear codes. The *New York Times* published a baseless claim of an affair with a lobbyist. An *Atlantic* photographer used a strobe light and doctored photos to make him look evil. They treated my dad fairly all the way up until he was a threat to beat Barack Obama, and then they were vicious.

It's this viciousness that allowed Trump to rise. When, in back-to-back elections, the media depicted my father and Mitt Romney as people you should be scared to have as president, everyone tuned them out. My theory on Trump has always been that the media and Democrats cried "Wolf!" so often that when the actual wolf showed up, they didn't even have the vocabulary for it. If you say all Republicans are bad, eventually you get one who is genuinely bad—and no one will believe you.

Another thing that allowed Trump's rise was how consultants corrupted the GOP, training candidates to promise one thing without any intention of delivering on it. However low and vile you think political consultants can be, I'm here to tell you: it's so much worse. Consultants like Steve Schmidt, John Weaver, and Nicolle Wallace betrayed my father in gross ways. Today they invoke his name all the time, and every time they do, I wish it would make them gag as the traitors they are.

Part of the problem with consultants, like so many members of our rarefied political class, is that they stand for nothing. My father had real beliefs, as do I—in individual liberty, in limited government, in an America that honors her commitments and defends her allies.

Those beliefs are denigrated in our corporate media time and again. They dismiss Republican women in particular as being something that doesn't exist. Even though there are tens of millions of women who share my views, outside of Fox, there is not a single visibly pro-life, pro-gun woman on-air on any broadcast television station other than me. That's not an accident. It's on purpose. They'd rather pretend every conservative in America is a fat old white guy, when that isn't the case.

I'm one of the only pro-life women in all of the media anywhere except Fox. I'm treated like a complete radical on the issue. Even though about 50 percent of the country agrees with me, I'm seen as Serena from *The Handmaid's Tale*. Upon hearing that I wasn't pro-abortion, someone called me a handmaid. "What could I say?" I replied as Serena: "Blessed be the fruit."

This is one of the reasons conservative women threaten the Left so much. I saw it firsthand when my father chose Sarah Palin as his running mate. Those same consultants who boast about how upright they are today took every opportunity to betray and undermine Sarah, sometimes in disgustingly misogynistic ways. And why? Because she was talented, beautiful, populist, conservative, and represented a political future that would kick them to the curb.

Approaching the Trump years without letting his personal slights color my analysis was challenging for me. He's a vindictive man, and the animosity he had toward my father ran deep. At the same time, my father always taught me to respect the office of the presidency. As a conservative, I saw a lot of things as good steps during those four years. The impact on our courts can't be underestimated. The addition of Justice Brett Kavanaugh, and the experience he went through of extreme personal attacks and unverifiable allegations, radicalized many conservatives who thought that there was any remaining hope for bipartisanship. Justice Amy Coney Barrett is a hero for conservative women everywhere—and again, instead of applauding her achievement, the Left depicted her as bringing on a literal *Handmaid's Tale* in America.

Whenever I'm judging politicians, I strive to take the good with the bad, and see both for what they are—even as it feels like in the media, almost no one is able to do that.

Most of my Democrat friends never understood this. But for me, it's all about being politically realistic. My conservative, my pro-life, pro-gun, pro-family beliefs don't stop just because America elected Donald Trump. They became all the more important. And they have to be at the center of a Republican Party dedicated to true American greatness going forward.

What does this greatness look like? To me, it looks like an America that values her people, honors her commitments, and stands ready to defend the free world against the encroaching influence of communist China and authoritarian Russia.

Unfortunately, at least in the early going, it doesn't look like Joe Biden is doing that. He seems to be giving people the Obama foreign policy without Obama.

The truth at the center of Donald Trump's rise was that many Americans felt our greatness slipping away. They saw the hollowed-out Rust Belt, the explosion in drug abuse, the woke takeover of our academies, the brutally anti-American media, and the lawlessness on our southern border as marks of a nation on the decline.

And when they listened to their leaders, what they heard was: *Accept this decline. It's inevitable. Just go along with it. Your televisions will be big and cheap.*

They rejected that because they're Americans. We are proud people. Accepting decline isn't in our nature.

The lie at the center of Donald Trump's rise was that, as he liked to say, he alone could fix it. He didn't know the first thing about governing. He wasn't a statesman. He wasn't a leader. He was a guy who fell ass-backward into a job and was surprised by it and unprepared for it. He's the dog who caught the car.

Now, Democrats and their media allies are all saying that we're going to reset the clock. It'll be as if that 46.9 percent of Americans didn't give Trump the most votes a Republican has ever gotten. When Barack Obama won the presidency in 2008, he received sixty-nine million votes; Trump won in 2016 with *seventy-four million*. And we're going to pretend those four years under Trump didn't happen and go back to "normalcy"?

Yeah. Right.

People want to believe that with Joe Biden as president, the country will become less polarized, but to me, it looks like it might get even worse. Emily Ekins, the head of polling research at the Cato Institute, did one of the most revealing and important polls of 2020. Her research found that Americans, and particularly conservative Americans, are increasingly terrified to share their true beliefs in public. It's true, and I know so many people—including educated, accomplished people—who have told me they're too scared to say what they believe.

On *The View*, I try to be their voice—to say the things they think that they can't.

When I was younger, it was the liberals who were all about free speech. The ACLU and other organizations were all about pushing back against Jerry Falwell, Pat Robertson, and Tipper Gore on rap lyrics and music videos. But now liberals aren't that liberal anymore. They're beholden to a new hierarchy of identity politics that seeks to destroy those with whom they disagree.

Empowered by the social media corporations in Silicon Valley, the radical Left is dedicated to shutting down and eliminating conservative speech from the public square. Defending the police, the military, religion, tradition, history, and our American way of life is anathema to them.

Electing Joe Biden isn't going to change any of that.

A big part of why it won't change is that expressions of love for our country have become such an indication of partisanship. It shouldn't be this way. As has been said by many a Democratic consultant, the biggest mistake their party made was giving the Bible and the flag over to Republicans. But now it seems like those in the younger generation of Democrat politicians are fine with that. They think the flag is a symbol of oppression, of racism, of evil.

That's the opposite of how I see it.

One afternoon when I was sixteen, my father and I were out driving together through a particularly anonymous stretch of Arizona.

I gazed out the passenger side, took in the flat, dusty land stretching to the mountains in the distance, sighed, and said, "Arizona is so boring."

The car slowed down. I looked over at my father in the driver's seat and saw anger in his eyes as he pulled over on the shoulder of the road. He put the car in park and turned to face me.

"Boring?" he said, as if I had said something so preposterous, so offensive, that he wanted to make sure he'd heard me correctly. I didn't say anything, and so he continued:

"How about a little gratitude for Arizona? How about recognizing that Arizona is one of the best places in the world? How about some appreciation for the fact that you are lucky, blessed to be in the state of Arizona? How about some proper awe for the nature and the people and the work and the blood and the sweat that went into making Arizona? How about some reverence for those that came before you? Of all the terrible places and eras in which you could have been born, you had the great fortune to be born in modern-day America, surrounded by untold natural beauty, a family that loves you, and a great democracy! And you're saying it's boring."

His anger made a huge impression on me. I'd go on to make all sorts of mistakes in life, embarrassing ones that no politician wants their daughter to make. He was never furious about those. But the casual contempt for my birthplace? That set him off.

When he was in the Hanoi Hilton, one of my dad's fellow prisoners, Mike Christian, had sewed a messy but heartfelt version of an American flag into his jacket. They would hang it on the wall and quietly say the Pledge of Allegiance together every morning.

When the guards found out about this, they beat the hell out of Mike Christian as a lesson to all of them. My dad woke up in the middle of the night to see Mike, dimly lit by a hanging light bulb, his eyes swollen almost shut, working again with his bamboo needle at a piece of cloth, because he'd be damned if they weren't going to have a flag to salute in the morning.

Some people have reasons for why they won't stand and salute our flag. Some of those reasons may be real. Some of them seem like excuses. But I know what the flag meant to my father. I know what it means to my family. And I know what it means to me.

When I grew up and left my family's house, I took to hanging an American flag on the wall of my dressing room at work and one over the mantel of the home Ben and I share. And when my daughter grows up, she'll know why.

CHAPTER 13

THE DEPARTURE

On July 1, 2021, I announced live on-air that I was leaving *The View* after four years. My cohosts learned about my decision that morning, and the shock registered on their faces. I'd been talking to ABC's higher-ups for weeks about wanting to leave. Up until the week before, they were trying to convince me to stay and finish out the two years left on my contract. I told them it was too late—I had to get out.

I didn't get much sleep the night before the announcement. I kept going over the things I'd be saying on the show the next morning—and also, the things I would not be saying. I *would* be talking about what an incredible opportunity being on the show was, how much respect I had for my cohosts, and how much I'd learned from being there. But I would not mention that the way

I'd been treated on the show as the resident conservative, particularly upon my return from maternity leave, had made it impossible for me to stay.

This is the part you all want to know about, right? You want all the details about what happens when the cameras aren't on at *The View*. I'm not going to dish on every piece of drama that I witnessed. I had a lot of good memories on the show, and it was a privilege to be part of such an iconic piece of TV history. And yes, I know that most jobs in TV are stressful, being in a pressure-cooker environment, and that is to be expected.

But there's stuff that happens on *The View* that shouldn't be allowed. For whatever reason, there's a deep level of misogyny about the way *The View* is covered and written about in the media, where tabloids are always writing about the cohosts hating each other backstage. It's a self-fulfilling prophecy because the atmosphere of *The View* breeds drama: producers can't control hosts, manage conflict, or control leaking. My take on the show is that working on *The View* brings out the worst in people. I believe that all the women and the staff are working under conditions where the culture is so messed up, it feels like quicksand.

I don't know why that is. Maybe it's because there's no high-level oversight of the show from the network. ABC won't lay down the law when it comes to conduct at *The View*. We're like the network's crazy cousin. HR reports seem to fall on deaf ears, starting from years before I worked there. And as a result, people—both on camera and off—feel empowered to act however they like, and do whatever they want.

In my four years there, I was the target of plenty of shade—too much to even begin to recount—and then I also experienced more toxic, direct, and purposeful hostility.

When I first joined *The View* in 2017, I felt a maternal connection to Whoopi. She had made a promise to my father that she would look after me, and she kept her word for the first two years that I was on the show. The thing about Whoopi, though, is that she wields so much power in culture and television, and once she turns on you, it can create unfathomable tension at the table. I found her open disdain for me more and more difficult to manage as the years went on and it became more frequent. Occasionally, if the show's political discourse veered into territory that she found disagreeable, Whoopi would cut me off, sometimes harshly. Once, in the middle of a heated debate on live TV, Whoopi singled me out and said, "Girl, stop talking." It instantly trended on Twitter. And it really hurt. Another time she answered something I said by blurting out *"Okay"* in a tone that declared she was both baffled and disgusted by what I had just said. This reaction also went viral and left a scar on our relationship. Day after day, week after week, these things took a toll.

You can't imagine how it messes with your self-esteem working in an environment where the worst thing you can be in the world is a Republican during the Trump years. As the country got worse under Trump, the treatment from Whoopi, Joy, and some of the staff grew meaner and less forgiving. It was as if I had become an avatar for everything they hated about the president. It felt like the cohosts and staff only knew one Republican—me—and took out all their anger on me, even though I didn't even vote for Trump.

It was hard for me to understand. And I couldn't explain it, because Whoopi and Joy saw front and center the emotional trauma that I experienced from President Trump's attacks on my family. There was more than one occasion when I had to go on live TV and address the next disgusting thing Trump was saying about my father, as my dad was sick.

After my dad died, I heard Joy had told others at *The View* that she couldn't understand how I could still defend Republicans after everything Trump had done to me. Why was that something she had to worry about? I could separate the two. I could separate Trump from being a Republican. And by the way, that was my job on the show. It's also how the great political analysts survive the ups and downs of each administration. *The View* wouldn't have had the ratings it did during my four years if I was like the conservative cohosts who succeeded Elisabeth Hasselbeck. Those women agreed with everyone and nodded politely. The women who once voted Republican and came to find nothing except the ability to trash the party and its members at every possible opportunity.

During my time on *The View*, I felt like I was often being punished and singled out for being a conservative. I'd hear a lot of complaints that the staff, including the other cohosts and producers, had problems with my "personality."

Until I got pregnant, I could handle it and manage it. No matter how hard the days were, I accepted the trade-off. I was on the most-watched TV show on daytime television with a platform to speak to—and for—millions of women in this country. This was the deal with the devil I knowingly made.

What changed was how I was treated after I had a baby. After I gave birth to Liberty, I suffered from severe postpartum anxiety. For those of you who don't know what this is, postpartum anxiety is a cousin to postpartum depression that affects about 10 percent of new moms, according to the American Pregnancy Association. The telltale signs are excessive worrying, racing thoughts, and feelings of dread. Where it turns from being different from normal new mom worries is the point at which it becomes irrational. I sadly had this in spades. I was paranoid that someone was going to kidnap Liberty to the point that I considered hiring armed bodyguards outside our house. I was afraid people wanted to kill her, or steal her or hurt her in some way. Every night, when she went to sleep, I would go in and check on her to make sure she was still breathing and still in her crib. As I was dealing with my own emotions, I couldn't also navigate the idea that I was hated and felt hated at a toxic work environment. The second that feeling set in, it started to snowball into me thinking that everyone hated me. And because of that, I was worried even more that someone would steal or kidnap my child—as a way of hurting me. It wasn't rational; I know that. But it was the medical diagnosis I was going through.

When I was getting ready to return to work, I told my producers that it was going to be rough for me. I didn't ask for special treatment, but I didn't expect the attacks to start either. When other women come back from maternity leave on *The View*, they are welcomed with confetti and baby presents. Also, I had been gone for three months and I had assumed they had missed seeing me. I was wrong.

On my second day back, as I was still getting my sea legs back and adjusting to my new schedule and life between breast-pumping and researching for my Hot Topics, Joy and I began squabbling a bit about the state of the Democratic Party on-air. To make light of things and to ease the tension, I said, "Joy, you missed me so much when I was on maternity leave! You missed fighting with me!"

"I did not," Joy said. "I did not miss you. Zero."

Nothing anyone has ever said to me on camera since I have been giving interviews, since I was twenty-two years old, has ever hit this hard. I felt like I'd been slapped. She yelled out at me sharp and intensely and I believed her. Now, I know I'm not always a perfect angel, but I would never speak to any woman that way who had just returned after giving birth. There are some things in life, and some moments in life, which are sacred. There are also times in life where you aren't as strong as you usually are.

"That's so nasty," I said, unable to hide my shock. "That's so rude."

Until that moment, it hadn't even occurred to me that Joy hadn't missed me. She'd texted me to see a baby picture of Liberty, and she had seemed happy for me. We'd chatted in a friendly way. I believed that, despite all our differences, deep down, we had a mutual understanding of respect for each other.

When we broke for commercial, I burst into tears. Not just like tearing up—uncontrollable sobbing. I was super hormonal and deeply hurt.

"If you guys didn't want me to come back, I wouldn't have come back!" I said to my producer in my earpiece. I told him he might need to pull my camera away for a minute because I wasn't sure if I could get myself together in time to go back to interviewing people.

I felt my breasts begin to leak from lactation. I was embarrassed and shaking. I felt like I wasn't in control of my body. And I didn't want millions of viewers to see that.

After sobbing for what felt like an eternity, I wiped my face, took deep breaths, and double-checked that my nipples were not in camera range. I tried to smile and focus as the show resumed.

The experience of crying and leaking and trying to pull it together in seconds so I could go back on-air with women who appeared to hate me was an intensely heartbreaking experience. I can't explain it further other than I felt like in that moment I took a look at my life outside of myself and I thought clearly, *This* shit *isn't worth this. Nothing in life is worth this.* I made it through the rest of the show and, afterward, I went into my office. Because of COVID, I taped the show in an almost empty ABC bureau office where it was just me and my makeup artist and our sound lady. They are lovely people, and we got along well, but I rushed downstairs, closed my door, threw up in a garbage can, and I finished the crying session I'd had to interrupt before. She'd triggered my postpartum anxiety and now I was on a roller coaster that I couldn't stop. While I cried, I no longer felt safe working at *The View.* It is one of the most singular feelings of loneliness and anguish I have ever felt in my entire life. It was a perfect storm of hormones, postpartum anxiety, and a lot of demons on *The View* coming out to bite me.

Later, I asked my executive producer for an apology from Joy. She had humiliated me live on-air and an apology from her didn't seem like a lot to ask. I was told I would not be getting one and we all just needed to move on. I never talked to Joy one-on-one again after that day.

Call me naïve, but when I came back to work after having a baby, I expected to be treated with respect. It had taken me so long to get healthy again. I'd had postpartum preeclampsia in the hospital, which is when you have scarily high blood pressure after giving birth. I couldn't breathe. I could barely stand up. I needed my husband and my sister-in-law to help me eat and walk. It was mortifying. When I took Liberty to her first pediatrician appointment, the doctor gave me a form to fill out about how I was coping. I failed it. I was shocked. The pediatrician pulled me aside and told me I needed to talk to my OB-GYN right away. My OB-GYN prescribed me Zoloft for my anxiety and I started going to therapy.

The View is billed as being honest and open. It's billed as an arena for women to share and discuss their views on politics and the most important topics of the day—an arena historically occupied by men. A space where women support—and respectfully challenge—each other. But the truth is that the environment on the show is toxic. Here I was, thinking that I had been through so much with these women. Together, we had helped bring the show back from the dead. We won an Emmy. We became America's "most-watched daytime talk show." We were on the covers of magazines. After giving birth, I did not feel like myself. I felt extremely vulnerable. Joy seemed to smell that vulnerability like a shark smells blood in the water, and she took after it. Why was this worth it to her? I will never know. But so much for working moms looking out for each other.

I realize *The View* is a TV show. I know what I signed up for. I am not some delicate flower. *The View* has a long, storied history that has been well documented. But up until the day I returned to work, I'd been in quarantine and completely isolated with a new baby. COVID pregnancy and my COVID fourth trimester was challenging, isolating, scary, intense, and liberating. When it was time to go back to work, I understood why women might not have children if they want to focus on their career. I was made to feel that my having a baby had inconvenienced everyone and that becoming a mother had made me weak. This beautiful thing that had happened in my life had turned into a shitty tabloid drama. And it *was* a shitty tabloid drama. That moment blasted across the internet and television media like a comet. Ultimately it proved too difficult for me to forgive or to move on from—especially because I was told I would not be getting an apology. I just didn't have the emotional bandwidth to try with any of them anymore. I thought I was part of a show where women can have the kinds of conversations that society doesn't generally make space for women to have. But, for me, *The View* no longer felt like a pro-women show. Soon after I returned, it hit me: I didn't want to be a part of it, for myself, for my daughter, and for women everywhere.

In the days after my return on *The View*, my postpartum anxiety got worse.

I became even more worried someone would try to hurt Liberty to punish me.

I had a hard time letting anyone else hold her but me.

I would have panic attacks taking her in a stroller because I was afraid someone would push me down and run off with her.

My husband, Ben, was very honest with my doctor and said, "She's having a hard time—it's more than depression." Two of my friends, Clay and Josh, told me I'd never seemed more anxious in all the years they'd known me. I know that many of you noticed it, too. I would hear from viewers saying that I looked so sad on *The View* in the winter of 2021.

I'd been unhappy at *The View* for a long time. My unhappiness was like this giant wave that had been building and building and finally crashed after I returned from leave. I don't think most people understand how all-consuming the show is. It's not like being a news host or a talking head. You're expected to share every detail of your life, and live in this quasi-reality TV existence, where you are constantly reacting to your TV family that may or may not hate you. Sometimes I would go home and start relaxing and unwinding and just catching my breath and the show's publicist would call me and say, "There's an article about you on *Page Six* or *TMZ* saying you're Axl Rose and you set the studio on fire and everybody hates you, and you're a monster and nobody wants you here."

You can shrug it off for a while—and I did—but at a certain point it starts to cause harm. It got to the point where I would arrive at the studio, get in the elevator alone, walk as fast as I could to my dressing room, and shut the door. I was so paranoid that any interaction I had could be sold to the press or become fodder on Twitter. Conversations could be taken out of context and used against me. I remember when I got there, one of the first stories was that I'd had a psychotic breakdown and was yelling about being the only Republican on the show. A version of that did happen, but not in the way it was reported. Something serious happened—I can't remember what—and I did yell that I was the only Republican on the show. But there was no "psychotic breakdown." One of the oldest tricks in the book is calling women crazy. If you have an emotional reaction to something mean they've done, they turn around and say, "She's so crazy. Look at her. What an unhinged lunatic!" There's no way to win because you're made to feel crazy and then you start going crazy. And when you go crazy, they say, "She's always been a basket case. Look at her! What a maniac." It wasn't like that for the other cohosts. They could have their emotions. They could get fired up about what they believed in. But I couldn't. I have endless stories about my colleagues' behavior on set and off. It's an emotional show and sometimes what happens backstage isn't pretty. But for some reason, it was always my stuff that leaked.

It started to feel very isolating.

Look, it's not all bad. I'll be attached to it for the rest of my life, for better or worse. I'm not mad about what happened to me. Other hosts who've left are like, "Fuck *The View*." I don't feel that way. I'm not bitter or angry. I want change. The idea of a show dedicated to women having conversations that society reserves for men is important and necessary in our culture. But there are some things about the show that feel stuck in 1997 when *The View* first went on-air. In this era of dismantling toxic work environments and refusing to accept the poor treatment of employees, how is *The View* still immune?

My experiences at *The View* made me think about how women are treated in the workplace, period. I want ABC to change. But I also want change in America, too, starting with giving pregnant women paid maternity leave. Corporations should not be allowed to say, "We support women, blah blah blah, but if you have a baby, we're not going to support you." These companies spend millions of dollars a year trying to convince consumers of their high moral values, but how many of them actually walk the talk? It needs to change.

I believe that ABC News should offer paid family leave to *all* employees.

I realize, too, that not all conservatives believe in paid family leave. This is a problem. Conservatives are supposed to be so pro-family, but too often their policies stop short of protecting and supporting women. I see this as one of my big issues, and this is a call to arms. I'm hopeful that being open and vulnerable with my story will help. Of course, I can't imagine what it's like for women who are less privileged than I am, women who work minimum-wage jobs, and single mothers struggling to make ends meet. But I do know how hard it was for me. And I'm sure it's much, much more difficult for them. I can't imagine how I would have gotten through that period of time in my life without the support from my friends and family and the resources of the amazing doctors and specialists who helped me come out the other side. Every woman should have the same access and resources I did in one of the most vulnerable and difficult times in a woman's life. I feel like we are collectively failing new moms and women in general in this country.

The morning I announced that I was quitting *The View*, I was exhausted because I didn't sleep at all the night before. I was so distracted leaving the house that I forgot my on-air clothes and coffee. When I realized I didn't have my coffee, I asked my Uber driver to stop so I could run into a coffee shop to get some.

I had been thinking about how my father had told me to take the job at *The View*. I don't think he was wrong, but I think he would have wanted me to go now. I helped the show win an Emmy. I buried him and showed up to work right after. I interviewed Donald Trump Jr., even though he'd attacked my family. I did everything that was asked and put my mental and emotional well-being aside for it.

When my dad died, it was a wake-up call about how little time we have. I felt like I didn't listen to that wake-up call, and then COVID happened, and now I feel like I *am* listening to it. Since COVID, a lot of people, but especially people my age, are reassessing what they want and what they consider worthwhile. My generation would rather make less money and create quality work, or do something they love, or work with people they respect. I never thought I was that person. But when I went back to the show, I felt like I was being disingenuous. I thought of the press I would have to do next season, the junkets. It's all about women supporting women. I didn't want to lie anymore. I couldn't. I couldn't put on the happy face after what I went through. Unlike a lot of women my age with little kids, *I* can afford to leave a toxic workplace. This is the great luxury of my life—being able to get up and leave when I've had enough. I know that makes me extremely privileged, and I feel heartsick for all women who feel trapped in places they can't afford to leave.

I was really mad and upset at myself for not being stronger when I got back to work. I felt as if I had failed. I thought to myself, *This is why people don't have children.* Now, when I see any woman who's pregnant or postpartum, all I want to say is, "What do you need? And how can I help you?" I never want to work for anyone again who doesn't look out for new mothers.

As I walked into the coffee shop on Capitol Hill, I heard the ABBA song "Take a Chance on Me" playing really loud. The people behind the counter were dancing to the song, smiling and laughing. ABBA was one of my dad's favorite bands. I felt like it was a sign from him: I was making the right decision.

EPILOGUE

THE RETURN

★ ★ ★

Before having Liberty, I thought everyone was full of it when they talked about how great it was to have a baby. I suspected that they were being saccharine to cover up their frustrations and that, if they were honest, they'd admit that they missed their freedom. The media made it seem that if you had a baby, your career would end. And I was turned off by the faux perfection of mommy blogs. Now, if anything, I feel like people undersold motherhood.

Liberty has changed everything. It's hard on my ego to admit it, but I was completely wrong about the whole thing. I now know that every cliché about having a baby is entirely accurate. My whole life, I've always hated waking up early. But it turns out I don't mind waking up early with her. She needs to be fed around 7:00 a.m., and when I lean over her crib, I see her so happy and so excited to greet another day. You can't help but be in a good mood when you see that.

"Good morning, babe!" I say. She smiles a huge smile and starts kicking and reaching up for me. Those moments are so beautiful, they cut you down at your knees. I scoop her up into my arms and put on music. Then I nurse her and talk to her and sing to her as she coos back. We look into each other's eyes, and we have whole conversations. I feel the same sense of peace, that same primal happiness, that I felt drinking coffee in the morning on the deck in Sedona with my dad.

Looking at Liberty, I see the history and future of my family, and I see a soul I was meant to nurture. I'm sure every mother feels this way, but for me, it was a shock to learn the truth of the saying that having a child is like suddenly having your heart outside your body.

When I was pregnant, my friend Kennedy said that the one consolation of having a parent die is that they meet souls in the afterlife and pick out your children for you. I thought she was crazy. Now I totally believe that's what happened. I can't explain it, but from her temperament to her mannerisms, I've become convinced that Liberty is 100 percent the baby I was meant to have. When she stares at a painting we have of my father, I think I can see recognition on her face.

She's wonderful in every way—the best thing I've ever done, easily, by far. As terrible as everything is out in the world, looking at her, I feel all the day's events slide into perspective.

"Are you surprised by how much I like being a mother?" I asked Ben the other night as Liberty slept on my chest.

"Yes," he said. "I'm surprised both that you're so good at it and that you like it so much."

I was always work-focused and self-focused, but that has all changed. She matters more to me than anything else, and now I want a million children. Even though this has been so hard—trying to work while feeding, pumping, and changing—I'm grateful for every moment.

The state of our country is another story.

My hopes for a return to normal have faded. I love people, I love being social, I love parties, I love friends, I love traveling. I am not a shy person, I love meeting new people, I love talking to people. All of that is gone now. I've been waiting for the pandemic to completely end, in increments of three months—"Surely by spring we'll be back to a semblance of normalcy . . ."; "Surely by summer . . ."—and now I'm beginning to wonder if we ever will.

The odds of my returning to New York City seem slimmer than ever. I finally made myself look through the boxes I shipped last spring from my apartment there to D.C.

Box after box held clothes from my former life as someone who regularly went to red-carpet events and formal occasions.

I called to donate a bunch of the clothes. The woman who came over to help me sort through them pulled out one item and asked, "Is this a funeral dress?"

"Yes," I said. "I did wear it to a funeral."

That happened several times, and each time, the sight of the garment took me right back to those awful days of going from one service to another, completely despondent. So many funerals. So many funeral dresses. The only one I kept was the one I wore when I gave the National Cathedral eulogy.

Getting rid of all those clothes felt profound, a confirmation that now I'm a different person, with different priorities. It felt like saying goodbye to my old life, and it felt like saying goodbye to another part of New York.

My feelings about my party have changed, too.

When dozens of Republicans reportedly gave QAnon conspiracy theorist and radical Marjorie Taylor Greene a standing ovation, I found myself thinking: *No wonder everybody thinks Republicans are crazy.*

On January 6, I cried watching the mob storm the Capitol. As Ben and I stared at the TV in our living room, it felt like we were living in a science-fiction movie. I've always respected authority, from firefighters to teachers to soldiers. To see police officers running for their lives, to see one murdered, five people dead by the end of the day—and the president and his followers doing nothing to stop it—chilled me to my core.

My sister-in-law works for Kevin McCarthy, the house minority leader. When she was able to return to the Capitol building, she found her office trashed, and a phone number scrawled on her desk. She wondered if the person who did that was hoping she'd call and ask him out. Instead, she gave the number to the FBI.

On January 7, I believed that either the Twenty-Fifth Amendment would be invoked or Trump would be impeached immediately. To me, this was an existential threat to our nation and our republic. But no. Even after all of that, more than a hundred Republicans voted against certifying the election results. And—as further proof that the party's values were out of whack—in Arizona, the GOP voted to censure my mother because she campaigned for Biden.

I wonder what the future will hold for the Republican Party. Just because Godzilla isn't stomping on buildings right this minute doesn't mean he's not still there under the water. That's how I feel about Trump. Just because he's not front and center doesn't mean he's gone. As I write this, Kevin McCarthy is getting ready to announce gangbusters, record-setting fundraising for Republican congressional races. Meanwhile, liberal members of the media are gloating about their 2020 victory. One of my cohosts recently said, "You with your trucks and your American flags . . ."

When people on the Left say things like that, it makes people in the middle of the country feel like you hate them. And you know what happens when they believe that you hate them? They vote for someone who says he loves them, whether that's Trump or whoever takes his place. Do you want a new incarnation of Trump? Because I sure don't. When I see people on CNN vilifying Tucker Carlson, I see them giving him power. Do they want to lay the groundwork for a Tucker Carlson presidency? Because I fear that's what they're doing.

I feel more intensely than ever that I must try to look to my father's example and to work with those whose views are different from my own. My impulse is to attack people who don't agree with me. In a way, it's what I feel I was born to do. I don't know how *not* to fight. And I have no other skills. It's too late, at this point, to go into real estate. This is the only thing I know how to do. But as a new mom and as someone so profoundly sad about the state of this country, I do believe I need to be part of the solution.

Every rational person I know is sad. The country is sick in so many ways—physically because of the virus, but also spiritually and emotionally. I'm still waiting for the tone shift now that Trump is gone, but I haven't seen it yet. We need real leadership. And we need to want to heal. As long as we're calling one another things like garbage, trash, deplorables, nothing will improve. I know it sounds cheesy, but we can't go on like this.

We have to be kinder to one another, and we have to place the blame for suffering where it belongs, not on the tens of millions of people we don't agree with.

I do work with veterans charities, and I see how much more we need to do to help them. According to the VA, seventeen veterans take their own lives each day.

During the pandemic, poor children without internet access lost an entire year of their education at a time in our country where our education system is already failing.

There's so much we're not looking at and we're not taking care of. So, of course, millions of people were willing to believe that only Trump would tell them the truth.

Whether in Brownsville or Appalachia, we don't do right by the poor. We're not even trying.

When January 6 happened, I just kept thinking: *We have failed these people.*

Everyone who took part in that violence should be in jail for the rest of their lives. They are domestic terrorists, and I hate all forms of terrorism. But this is going to keep happening unless we do something to make people on the margins feel invested in this country.

There is so much to do: tackling the opioid crisis, prison reform, more forgiveness, leading with love in conversations—which I'm certainly trying to do more of now.

Having children requires you to be hopeful about the future. You're living for the benefit of someone you hope will outlive you.

Becoming a mother has made me understand my father better, too. I know why he was so sad to leave us. Now, when I pray, I pray to God and also to my dad. I ask both for advice. My father answers my existential questions more directly. It still feels like he's with me, just in a different form.

As I write this, Liberty is laughing, grabbing at everything, and trying to roll over. When she's on her stomach, she pushes up and grunts like she's in a gym doing yoga. She wants to be around me and to be involved in whatever's happening, whether it's a Zoom meeting or a meal. She's happiest when she's in the middle of any animated conversation. For me, she is the antidote to everything terrible—a light in the darkness of this year's tragedies.

What will the world be like for her? I just want her to be proud of me. I want to do work and put things out in the world that she can be proud of. I want to foster a new environment and a new world that she will want to exist in. There's no other option anymore except to work together to make things better. If we haven't hit rock bottom, surely we are close. There's only one thing left to do. When you're going through hell, you have to keep going.

ACKNOWLEDGMENTS

Thanks, of course, to Ben and Liberty, for their love and for being the reason I do everything I do. And to my fantastic friends, especially Josh, Clay, Jeisohn, Grant, Ramin, Kat, Hassim, and Abby.

Thanks to my brother Jimmy for being my therapist, and to my sister-in-law Emily for being my rock, my mother for being such an inspiration, and my sister Bridget for always being my support.

Thanks to the women of *The View*, and to everyone I've been lucky enough to work with and learn from in media over the years, my producer Daniella Greenbaum, and my assistant Molly Kessler.

I am lucky to have a great team: my agent, Max Stubblefield; publicist, Christophe Hollocou; lawyer, Roger Grad; and my chosen big sister, Laurye Blackford.

For her help keeping this project on track, thank you to Ada Calhoun, an angel sent from heaven!

For his patience and wisdom, I am indebted to my editor, Andrew Eisenman. Also, thank you to his whole crew at Audible.

INDEX

Martin, Jonathan, 59
The Masked Singer, 147
maternity leave, as bipartisan issue,
40–41
Matthews, Chris, 154
Mattis, Jim, 77, 120
Mayo Clinic, 46, 107
McCain, Andy, 65
McCain, Bridget, 43, 65, 73
McCain, Carol, 65, 66
McCain, Cindy, 95, 106
McCain, Doug, 65
McCain, Holly, 75, 76
McCain, Jack, 65
McCain, Jimmy, 65, 123, 132
McCain, John. *see also* election of
2008
  career advice to Meghan, 47–48
  death of, 71–78
  diagnosis and illness, 46–47,
  63–69
  eulogy, 89–100, 200
  as father, 79–84
  funeral services, 85–100, 119
  and Meghan's wedding, 107–110
  military service, 69, 82–83, 93,
  95, 182
  and Barack Obama, 148
  portrayal in media, 153, 176–177
  as prisoner of war, 82, 93, 95,
  182
  relationship with Meghan, 142,
  148–150, 181–182, 203
  respect of, for women, 143–144
  and Donald Trump, 45, 120,
  158–162, 186
McCain, Meghan. *see also*
  Domenech, Ben; *The View*
  at Catholic school, 79, 166
  college campus speaking
  engagements, 123–129
  courtship and marriage, 101–115
  departure from *The View,*
  183–196
  and election of 2008, 141–142,
  148–156
  friends of, 116–122
  maternity leave of, 2, 39–44
  political beliefs, 3–4, 177–178
  pregnancy and motherhood,
  7–25, 26–44, 197–199
McCain, Roberta, 143–144
McCain, Sidney, 65
"McCain Blogette," 146
McCarthy, Kevin, 200–201
McWhorter, John, 129
Meacham, Jon, 151–153
Medal of Honor, 148
Meet the Press, 55
Meghan's Cactus (Instagram feed),
16
Meyers, Seth, 7–11, 13–15
Michaels, Lorne, 10
Minneapolis, Minn., 140
Minutemen (border patrol), 129
Mississippi, 114
MSNBC, 9, 144, 154–155
MTV, 149
Muskogee, Okla., 143
Myspace, 149

N
NAFTA (North American Free
Trade Agreement), 115
National Institutes of Health
(NIH), 64
National Review, 166
National Rifle Association (NRA),
176
Nation of Islam, 57
Native Americans, 74, 77, 160
Navajo culture, 74
NBC, 155
Netanyahu, Benjamin, 175

ABOUT THE AUTHOR

Meghan McCain is a former co-host of ABC's *The View*, which she joined in October of 2017. While at *The View*, the show rose to new heights earning two daytime Emmy nominations for Outstanding Entertainment Talk Show Host. As the daughter of the late Senator John McCain, Meghan has been steeped in the high-stakes political arena since childhood. Often said to possess the McCain "maverick gene," Meghan has no qualms about saying what is on her mind, bragging that she inherited "my dad's heart-burn-inducing ability to say what he thinks." A powerful, singular role model for women and Republicans alike, McCain passionately discusses women's issues, social issues, and LGBTQIA equality.

Prior to joining *The View*, McCain was a co-host on the after-noon talk program *Outnumbered* on the Fox News Channel. She was also a co-host on Pivot TV's late night news program *TakePart Live*. McCain was also the creator, executive producer and host of the genre-busting docuseries *Raising McCain* which also aired on Pivot. The series followed the outspoken McCain on the road, talking to unexpected experts and everyday people by exploring a range of topics from bullying and feminism to sex overload and the death of romance, among others.

Raised in Phoenix, Arizona, McCain graduated from Columbia University with a degree in Art History. With ambitions to pursue a career in music journalism, she completed internships at *Newsweek* and *Saturday Night Live* before joining her father's 2008 presidential campaign where she launched a blog that gained an avid readership almost immediately (the blog received two distinguished awards in politics, The Golden Dot Award for Best Blog, and two Pollie Awards from the Association of Political and Public Affairs Professionals). She then burst onto the national media scene as a columnist for *The Daily Beast* and an MSNBC contributor. A *New York Times* best-selling author, McCain wrote and published her first book, *Dirty Sexy Politics* in 2010 followed by a children's book, both of which were inspired by her time on the campaign trail during her father's Presidential run. McCain's third book recounts the cross-country road trip that she and liberal comedian Michael Ian Black embarked upon together in 2011.